Cambridge Ele

Elements in Religion and
edited by
Paul K. Moser
Loyola University Chicago
Chad Meister
*Affiliate Scholar, Ansari Institute for Global Engagement with Religion,
University of Notre Dame*

MONOTHEISM IN CHRISTIAN LITURGY

Joris Geldhof
KU Leuven

CAMBRIDGE
UNIVERSITY PRESS

CAMBRIDGE
UNIVERSITY PRESS

Shaftesbury Road, Cambridge CB2 8EA, United Kingdom

One Liberty Plaza, 20th Floor, New York, NY 10006, USA

477 Williamstown Road, Port Melbourne, VIC 3207, Australia

314–321, 3rd Floor, Plot 3, Splendor Forum, Jasola District Centre,
New Delhi – 110025, India

103 Penang Road, #05–06/07, Visioncrest Commercial, Singapore 238467

Cambridge University Press is part of Cambridge University Press & Assessment,
a department of the University of Cambridge.

We share the University's mission to contribute to society through the pursuit of
education, learning and research at the highest international levels of excellence.

www.cambridge.org
Information on this title: www.cambridge.org/9781009001847

DOI: 10.1017/9781009003896

First published 2023

A catalogue record for this publication is available from the British Library.

ISBN 978-1-009-00184-7 Paperback
ISSN 2631-3014 (online)
ISSN 2631-3006 (print)

Cambridge University Press & Assessment has no responsibility for the persistence
or accuracy of URLs for external or third-party internet websites referred to in this
publication and does not guarantee that any content on such websites is, or will
remain, accurate or appropriate.

Monotheism in Christian Liturgy

Elements in Religion and Monotheism

DOI: 10.1017/9781009003896
First published online: January 2023

Joris Geldhof
KU Leuven

Author for correspondence: Joris Geldhof, joris.geldhof@kuleuven.be

Abstract: In line with a profound theological understanding of liturgy as the Church at prayer (*ecclesia orans*), the focus of this Element is the variegated ways in which Christians address, turn to, and worship God in their central rituals and celebrations. Surveying a representative sample of official liturgical sources from different Christian Churches, the question is asked how "pure" the monotheism expressed in them is. For one could argue that there is some ambiguity involved, especially with respect to (i) the peculiar position of Christ, the Son of God, and God the Father in liturgical prayers, and (ii) regarding the veneration of the saints. The essential key to unlock this complex and multi-layered reality is a meticulous study of the essential doxological nature of Christian liturgy, both from a phenomenological point of view and on the basis of fine textual analyses.

This Element also has a video abstract: www.cambridge.org/geldhofmonotheism

Keywords: Christian liturgy, doxology, worship, Christ as Lord, liturgical prayer

ISBNs: 9781009001847 (PB), 9781009003896 (OC)
ISSNs: 2631-3014 (online), 2631-3006 (print)

Contents

Introduction

This Element investigates the central importance of the Christian conviction that there is only one God, not many, and does that from a deliberate and distinctive *liturgical* perspective. In particular, it will be shown how this idea profoundly permeates the liturgical life of the Church. The leading hypothesis undergirding the present investigations is that faith in the existence of one God is not primarily an epistemological theory or an ontological statement, but a doxological and soteriological reality. In other words, monotheism as established by the liturgy of Christians first and foremost serves the worship of one true Savior. It is because of the unique and universal saving activity of Christ, which is the apex of the history of salvation as well as the center of gravity of the economy of salvation, that God is acknowledged, venerated, and explicitly addressed as the only one *worthy of worship*.

Before investigating anything in greater detail, it is important to elucidate the particular understanding of Christian liturgy which lies at the basis of this Element and which, as a consequence, runs through it. On purpose, it is a "thick" or "robust" and, consequently, profoundly *theological* understanding of liturgy, to be contrasted with a merely descriptive or empirical approach. It ties in with the model of liturgical theology as it was developed by Alexander Schmeman and Aidan Kavanagh.[1] This means that it sees the liturgical tradition as the "ontological condition" for theologizing.[2] More than a merely practical field where theoretical principles are applied, be they doctrinal, pastoral or canonical in nature, liturgy is the foundational reality giving shape to the Christian religion in its entirety. It is the privileged place where the communion of the faithful constantly renews its connection with God. It is the place where the communion with God is established and commemorated, where it is nourished, and where it is expressed and communicated.

In the famous words of the Second Vatican Council, liturgy is the "the summit toward which the activity of the Church is directed; at the same time it is the font from which all her power flows."[3] Or, as it is often repeated in more concise wordings, liturgy is the "source and summit" of the life of faith, in which the

---

[1] For a survey of the field of liturgical theology, see Joris Geldhof, "Liturgical Theology," *Oxford Research Encyclopedia of Religion* (2015): https://oxfordre.com/religion/view/10.1093/acrefore/9780199340378.001.0001/acrefore-9780199340378-e-14.

[2] Aidan Kavanagh, *On Liturgical Theology* (Collegeville: Liturgical Press, 1992), 75; Alexander Schmemann, "Theology and Liturgical Tradition," in *Liturgy and Tradition: Theological Reflections of Alexander Schmemann*, ed. Thomas Fisch (New York: Saint Vladimir's Seminary Press, 1990), 18. For a more extensive exposé of Schmemann's position, see his groundbreaking study *Introduction to Liturgical Theology*, trans. Asheleigh E. Moorehouse (Crestwood: Saint Vladimir's Seminary Press, 2003 [1966]).

[3] *Sacrosanctum Concilium*, #10.

Eucharist occupies the central position,[4] from which it ramifies into every element, component, and dimension of which it consists. The liturgy constitutes that to which, ultimately, every thought and action of Christians should be directed, while it at the same time motivates, stimulates, and inspires everything they undertake.

Clearly, this understanding of liturgy does not content itself with phenomenological circumscriptions of the rituals, ceremonies, and prayer services held by Christians. It requires a thorough theological engagement. A somewhat unusual, but very apt, definition of liturgy is the one proposed by American theologian David Fagerberg, a scholar whose work has to be situated in the wake of Schmeman's and Kavanagh's. The definition Fagerberg has come up with after long reflection and which he further develops in his oeuvre is as follows: "Liturgy is the perichoresis of the Trinity kenotically extended to invite our synergistic ascent into deification."[5]

What is striking about this definition is the absence of any vocabulary linked with social sciences and anthropology, such as the concepts of ritual, assembly, or communal action. Instead, Fagerberg opts for weighty theological notions with a significant history and multilayered meanings – perichoresis, Trinity, kenosis, synergy, ascent, and deification or theosis – and puts them in an intriguing cohesion. Also the verbs that are used in his definition, to extend and to invite, are noteworthy, since they quite rightly suggest that the liturgy is an open and dynamic operation.

Even if the concept of monotheism is not explicitly used in Fagerberg's definition, the definition itself is highly relevant for the purposes of this Element. One reason monotheism does not occur in the definition is because the term itself is rather a theoretical construction to label the specificity of an image of God in particular religions, among which is Christianity, than a concept sprouting forth from the continued effort of theologians to come to terms with the mystery of God's revelation in history. Yet this latter aspect is clearly present in Fagerberg's definition. It makes one understand that liturgy is all about sharing or participating in a transformative process of liberation anchored in God's self-emptying. It expresses the core Christian belief that God became human so that humankind can reach, and ultimately be reconciled with, the one God who took the initiative for this unique and universal salvation.

Hence, liturgy can be said to be at the crossroads of receiving and passing on God's liberating Word and, in and through that, divine grace and salvation. It is situated in the grand adventure of God's people throughout the times. In a way,

---

[4] See also *Lumen gentium*, #11.
[5] David W. Fagerberg, *Consecrating the World: On Mundane Liturgical Theology* (Kettering: Angelico Press, 2016), 6.

liturgy *is* the journey that starts from and ends in God, as it is sometimes expressed by means of the medieval *exitus-reditus* schema.[6] All of this supposes, however, that there is only one God and, thus, only one economy of salvation, once and for all, from now until the end of times.

Of course, every definition has its limits. In spite of its theological profundity and expressiveness, such is also the case for Fagerberg's definition of liturgy. It is not that it is wrong – on the contrary – but it lacks a crucial dimension, inasmuch as it does not explicitly refer to the reality of the Church. The Church is understood here as the receptacle of the Trinity's kenotic extension and as the place where the collaborative ascent toward theosis takes place. Concretely, this happens through sets of human actions and activities performed by a community, the Church.

There are good reasons to assume that the central, or most essential, activity of the Church is prayer. Key representatives of the Liturgical Movement in the twentieth century consistently proposed to fundamentally consider liturgy as the praying Church, that is, the Church which sees it as its most important task to render God the most appropriate praise. So it comes as no surprise that "the Church 'at prayer'" is yet another definition of liturgy, in this case a very famous one in the field of liturgical studies.[7] The notion has obvious references to the Latin phrase *ecclesia orans*.[8] This concise phrase adequately expresses the idea that liturgy and Church mutually imply each other. Neither can there be Church without liturgy, nor can there be liturgy without Church. And the activity of prayer is what binds the two together.

The challenge of this Element is to show (i) how Fagerberg's theological definition of liturgy matches with the more classical ecclesiological understanding of liturgy typical of the Liturgical Movement, and (ii) how the liturgy hence constitutes a paramount resource to examine the peculiar monotheistic beliefs

---

[6] It was the French Dominican scholar Marie-Dominic Chenu who developed the idea that the order implicit in Thomas Aquinas' *Summa Theologiae* was one of *exitus* and *reditus*. Chenu argued that, according to Thomas, everything flows forth from God and that everything also ultimately returns to God. Even if Aquinas did not purposely organize his *Summa* in this way, there is wide agreement that this interpretation scheme of Chenu is accurate and that it helps understand the underlying rationale of the *Summa*. See Brian Davies, *Thomas Aquinas's* Summa Theologiae: *A Guide and Commentary*(Oxford: Oxford University Press, 2014), 14–15. An argument could be set up that Christian liturgies are always to some extent caught up between an *exitus* from and a *reditus* to God. Christian liturgy has indeed a fundamental katabatic and anabatic dynamic.

[7] James D. Crichton, *Christian Celebration: The Prayer of the Church* (London: Geoffrey Chapman, 1976).

[8] In this context a reference ought to be made to the famous handbook of liturgy developed by Aimé-Georges Martimort, the original French title of which was *L'église en prière*, translated into English as *The Church at Prayer*. Also, it is no coincidence that the journal of liturgical studies published by the Pontifical Liturgical Institute at Sant'Anselmo in Rome is called *Ecclesia Orans*. Previously, the same title was used for a renowned book series in the Germanophone world.

of Christians. The guiding hypothesis is that it is both interesting and meaning-ful to look at the liturgical practices of Christian Churches in order to gain a better insight into how monotheism really works in Christianity.

This hypothesis will be tested in confrontation with two clusters of liturgical practice where this monotheism seems less evident. On the one hand, there is the question of the ultimate addressee of liturgical prayer. Obviously, this is God, but, at least at first sight, liturgical prayers may reveal some ambivalence as to whether God here means the Father, the Son, or the Spirit. In other words, the question is how established prayers in Christian liturgies manifest both the fundamental monotheistic conviction of Christians and their faith in a triune God. On the other hand, it seems that the widespread practice of the cult of the saints, in particular among Catholic and Orthodox Christians, constantly risks undermining the purity of Christians' monotheistic belief. In light of the manifold confusions that arise here, especially in the context of popular devo-tions, the question is how the veneration of the saints, and the underlying assumption of their close proximity to God, can be reconciled theologically with the exigencies of monotheism.

The choice to investigate both liturgical prayer formulae and a more cultic aspect of the Christian religion is deliberate. It is inspired by the idea that liturgy is a multifaceted and complex reality, the access to which cannot only consist of texts. In the area of liturgical studies and liturgical theology in particular, there is a growing consensus that liturgical reality has to be studied always from different perspectives and with the aid of not one but always several methods.[9] Moreover, liturgical prayers and ritual, cultic and devotional practices them-selves cannot be surgically separated. A phenomenological and theological argument can be unfolded that liturgy never consists of either prayer or rite, but that it always situates itself on the spectrum between both. Hence, since liturgies are always mixtures or combinations of prayer and ritual, theology must deal with them as such, that is, not deal with them as if they were examples of theoretical constructions.

In order to meet the challenges as set out above, and thus to investigate how the Christian liturgy manifests Christians' monotheistic faith, this Element is structured as follows. First, it is necessary to examine the abovementioned two different dimensions of liturgy, ritual and prayer, in greater detail, as well as the way in which they correspond with cult and faith. The elucidation of a certain tension between cult and faith will enable us to get a clearer picture of what monotheism means in the context of worship.

---

[9] For a substantial elaboration of that argument, see Joris Geldhof, *Liturgical Theology as a Research Program* (Leiden and Boston: Brill, 2020).

A second step will be to inquire into the basic doxological outline of liturgical prayer and to clarify how theology tries to express that. Third a discussion of concrete liturgical material from the Christian tradition follows, with the specific goal of examining how the oneness and uniqueness of God are imagined in a variety of doxological formulae. Fourth this line of inquiry is set forth in a discussion of the traditional formulae with which liturgical prayers close. In those closing formulae one can observe an intriguing ambiguity between the divinity of the Father and that of the Son, which raises interesting questions about how consistently monotheistic the liturgy is.

Whereas Sections 2–4 can be said to naturally connect to the prayer dimension of Christian liturgy, the fifth leans more toward its ritual dimension. Thus the fifth section of this Element sheds light on the veneration of the saints and in that cannot but make a special reference to the role of Mary. Of Mary, God's mother, one could say that "theologically speaking, her role is fundamentally mandated by the construction of the divine in monotheism as fostering both paternal and maternal modes of transmission."[10] Sometimes it is even suggested that Mary is the hidden female God of Christianity, thereby threatening the purity of monotheism of course, and calling into question its at least perceived inherent patriarchal infrastructure.[11] But it is not Mary only but all the saints who have supposedly posed a permanent threat to the Christian faith in one God.

1 Christian Liturgy as Cult and Faith

To guide us in the exploration of the double nature of liturgy as ritual and prayer, which is a vast topic in and of itself, a choice is made here to focus on one author whose work is particularly interesting for the purposes of this Element. His name is Antoon Vergote (1921–2013). A native of Kortrijk, a town in the west of Belgium near the French border, Vergote became a Roman Catholic priest of the diocese of Bruges. He was a renowned professor teaching courses at the faculties of psychology, philosophy, and theology of the Catholic University of Leuven for many years. He was an extraordinary scholar who had earned doctorates in both biblical exegesis and scholastic philosophy. In the late 1950s he moreover specialized in psychoanalysis at Paris, where he met with Jacques Lacan, Claude Lévi-Strauss, and Maurice Merleau-Ponty, among others. In his rich reflections in the area of the philosophy of religion the question of the biblical religion and its monotheism play a salient role.

---

[10] Cleo McNelly Kearns, *The Virgin Mary, Monotheism, and Sacrifice* (Cambridge: Cambridge University Press, 2008), 267.

[11] Geoffrey Ashe, *The Virgin: Mary's Cult and the Re-emergence of the Goddess* (London: Arkana, 1988).

However, Vergote's input will above all help us understand how culture, cult, and Christian faith interact.

In several of his later writings, Vergote is passionate to discern the specificity of Christianity. He concludes that, above anything else, this has to do with the love of God.[12] This love, however, must be very clearly understood, for it is in no way similar to a vague sense of attachment to a transcendent being of some kind. Such a sensitivity or general religiosity, Vergote submits, has hardly anything to do with Christianity. He explains his position by drawing fine distinctions between "religiosity without religion," "religious belief," and a "religion of faith."

According to Vergote, a religiosity without religion is what characterizes late modern cultures especially in Western Europe. It is comparable to what sociologists have described as "believing without belonging," an existential attitude of persons which makes them not necessarily downright atheistic but which nevertheless keeps them far away from an explicit and steady commitment to traditional religion, its representatives, and its institutions. This religiosity without religion is not per se negative, in the sense that it can take on the form of a great appreciation for the historical role of Christianity in Western societies, for the stunning art it produced, or for some key values, for example, of peace, harmony, perseverance, and solidarity, it promoted. References to God, however, are difficult to find in these discourses and, when they are found, they are usually to an impersonal deity. Within the confines of a religiosity without religion God has become a dimension, an energy, something unnamable, something beyond. Traditional religious celebrations are sometimes attended, but in general only for aesthetic reasons or out of a certain nostalgia. The celebrations may additionally arouse a spiritual feeling, but this usually gets suppressed soon afterward, when the busyness of ordinary life takes over the agenda again.

Put differently, a religiosity without religion does not subscribe to any religious beliefs, at least not to the extent that they are made explicit in distinctive narratives and doctrines, the formulations and contents of which are carefully watched over and defended by authoritative bodies. Religious beliefs, however, put an indelible mark on the identity of a religious community or tradition. They express contents with a certain appeal to truth, often connected with claims about the origin of everything and the sustenance of life, the social order, the cosmos, being itself, and so on. Religious beliefs are related to variegated stories about interactions and exchanges between humankind and deities. Vergote sees

---

[12] Antoon Vergote, *De Heer je God liefhebben: Het eigene van het christendom* (Tielt: Lannoo, 1999).

a particular connection between religious beliefs and myths. They structure the self-understanding of people belonging to a particular culture. As a consequence, their importance ought not to be underestimated.

Very important for Vergote, however, is that a clear difference is made between religious belief and religion of faith.[13] Christianity, for him, is fundamentally a, even *the*, religion of faith. Faith is what uniquely distinguishes Christianity among the religions of the world. It is not so much taking for granted certain convictions, living in accordance with a religiously motivated moral code, or adopting a set of stories in one's cultural, national, or personal identity. Rather, faith is rooted in a free assent to the invitation of an absolutely transcendent God to share in his glory, accept his grace, interiorize his Word, and live accordingly. In all of this a love of God prevails.[14]

Clearly, the Christian religion can take on the shape of being attached to stories inspiring identities, to doctrines upheld by ecclesiastical authorities, and to a distinctive ethical life. However, Vergote hypothesizes that these manifestations and beliefs are secondary to "faith," that is, the personal relationship with God. As a corollary, he is a sharp critic when he observes instances and circumstances where Christianity tends to become a religion among the religions. In all such cases, Vergote opines that it neglects its own foundation.

As a consequence, according to Vergote, it is of paramount importance not to confuse culture and religion. Many philosophical and anthropological theories suggest or accept that culture and religion co-originate. Vergote tends to agree with these theories if and inasmuch as they are not applied to Christianity and its Jewish origins without making necessary distinctions. The basis for these distinctions lies in the emergence of monotheism.

Vergote is convinced that a monotheistic image of God is not the result of a natural evolution or historical process. Monotheism is a discontinuity, irreducible to prior developments, not the result of some immanent law. It came as something "new" in the history and the consciousness of humankind. For Vergote the emergence of monotheism is linked with Semitic culture in the Ancient Near East, in particular with the figure of Moses,[15] but that it appeared at all in that specific context is as such contingent. Out of itself, philosophy cannot come up with the idea of a monotheistic faith. Its reasonability can only

---

[13] In passing it should be mentioned in this context that in Dutch it is not possible to hear the difference between "belief" and "faith." Both words are rendered with "geloof" (equal to "Glaube" in German). Hence Vergote consistently speaks about the contrast between "religieus geloof" and "geloofsreligie."

[14] Vergote, *De Heer je God liefhebben*, 175–187.

[15] Vergote, *De Heer je God liefhebben*, 52–60.

be shown afterward, a posteriori.[16] In other words, there are no a priori grounds on the basis of which one can accept or embrace monotheism. It has to be revealed and thus breaks with any previous forms of religion. Monotheism hence always equals a demythologization of sorts – which is the reason why Christianity could go along so well with Greek philosophy, Vergote surmises.

Monotheism has a couple of specific features, which Vergote highlights from a consistent phenomenological perspective.[17] That means that he brackets his personal faith and attempts at making a philosophical argument. The God of monotheism is first of all a personal God. He speaks to the prophets in person and does not reveal something but only himself. He reveals his will, his name, his holiness, his being. God moreover does not coincide with any natural force. His self, or inner life, is unrelated to anything within the world. He is absolutely transcendent, beyond time, fundamentally different, *other*. His being is unfathomable and inaccessible for the human mind, reason, and imagination. Not a single idea, concept, or name humans invent can do justice to God. However, God is also a God who engages with history. He is present in the world, among other things with an unfailing appeal to justice, mercy, and goodness. The least one can say about God is that He is not morally indifferent.

Applied to worship and liturgy, it is precisely God's absolute transcendence, out of which he breaks only for revealing himself, personhood, and profound commitment to humankind, which matter. These fundamental characteristics constitute the reasons to revere Him, to (try to) stay loyal to Him, to live from what He has to say (above anything else said by someone else), to be grateful to Him (in the first place), to honor Him (only) and to beg to be able to share in His (and no one else's) grace and glory. Christian liturgy must be understood as the ordered amalgamation of religious practices which make believers entertain the right attitude toward God in their lives. Its being cult and ritual must always be accompanied by, and even rest on, faith and prayer.

Another crucial concept in this context, making the connection between the transcendent God and the immanent liturgy, is *mystery*. Mystery derives its content from God's revelation and mediates it to humankind. Mystery functions as the hinge between God and history and thus offers humans access to divine revelation on a permanent basis – it is there always and everywhere. However, Vergote rightly points to the fact that the meaning of mystery in Christianity differs from the one it has in speculative thinking, where it simply refers to the limits of the capacity for conceptualizing. In Christian theology mystery is never something neutral. It is always qualified as mystery *of salvation*.

---

[16] Antoon Vergote, *Cultuur, religie, geloof* (Leuven: Universitaire Pers Leuven, 1989), 79.

[17] Vergote, *Cultuur, religie, geloof*, 88–93.

As such the mystery of salvation is "the expression that holds together the positive understanding of God's salvation initiatives with the consciousness of not being able to derive and explain them from general rational principles."[18]

Vergote does not refer to them, but it is worth noting at this point that liturgical theologians have developed a rich understanding of mystery which supports and can further elucidate what Vergote means. Among others, there was Odo Casel's influential theory of *Mysteriengegenwart*, arguing that liturgy constitutes above all a constant presence of God's saving mysteries. First and foremost, Casel contends with ample reference to the Bible, in particular the Pauline corpus, that mystery is "God considered in himself, as the infinitely distant, holy, unapproachable, to whom no man [*sic*] may draw near and live."[19] But, intriguingly, this divine mystery became incarnate. It became flesh in Christ. "Christ is the mystery in person, because he shows the invisible godhead in the flesh."[20] Liturgical celebrations, then, embody, express and offer the economy of salvation in the concrete history of people's life. It is the mystery of Christ, "what the apostles proclaimed to the Church, and what the Church passes on to all generations."[21]

In a similar vein, Cipriano Vagaggini held that "sacred history, mystery, mystery of Christ, mystery of the Church are indivisible, are even a single reality, so that we could actually speak of a single concept given different shadings by these various expressions."[22] The reason is that liturgy embodies through signs, symbols, rites, and prayers nothing but the economy of salvation, which is rooted in God's revelation and in the history in which aspects of that became apparent. Vagaggini accordingly maintains that "[i]n order to penetrate the world of the liturgy we must penetrate the world of revelation" and that "it is imperative to consider the liturgy always against the general background of sacred history,"[23] that is, the history of salvation.

Even if Vergote is not so explicit in the use of theological notions, one can say that there is a fundamental correspondence between what he says about revelation and what Casel and Vagaggini say about mystery. Revelation and mystery are essential categories to understand the Christian worship of God, personal and transcendent, one, unique and universal.

Two aspects of Vergote's thinking deserve some further treatment and clarification by way of a comparison with other authors who have said similar things.

---

[18] Vergote, *Cultuur, religie, geloof*, 93 (my translation, JG).

[19] Odo Casel, *The Mystery of Christian Worship*, ed. Burkhard Neunheuser (New York: The Crossroad, 1999), 5. The German original title of his work is *Das christliche Kultmysterium*.

[20] Casel, *The Mystery*, 6.   [21] Casel, *The Mystery*, 7.

[22] Cipriano Vagaggini, *Theological Dimensions of the Liturgy: A General Treatise on the Theology of Liturgy*, trans. Leonard J. Doyle and William A. Jurgens (Collegeville: Liturgical Press, 1976), 18.

[23] Vagaggini, *Theological Dimensions*, 3.

First, there is the remarkable emphasis on the figure of Moses as the initiator of biblical monotheism. Vergote's position here resembles Jewish scholar Yehezkel Kaufmann's (1889–1963) take on the matter. Kaufmann was an influential intellectual and specialist of the Bible and classical Hebrew in the crucial time frame before and after World War II. His research and philosophical views significantly impacted the academic world of Israel. His writings became much more widely known when a selection of them were compiled and translated into English in the early 1960s under the straightforward title *The Religion of Israel*.[24] Even if I have not been able to trace a direct influence of Kaufmann on Vergote, it is illuminating to evaluate the differences and similarities between them.

Kaufmann keenly defended the idea that Israel's monotheism is a unique invention of Israel to be connected with the figure of Moses and, thus, to be situated in history. Kaufmann considers Moses to be nothing less than "the initiator of a religious revolution."[25] This means that the monotheism of the biblical religion is not in line with other sociocultural and religious developments in the cultures of the Ancient Near East, as many scholars now, but also in Kaufmann's time, assume. For Kaufmann, it is of utmost importance to postulate a sharp difference between paganism and Israel's belief in one God. He describes the fundamental contents of that faith as follows:

> [T]he biblical religious idea, visible in the earliest strata, permeating even the "magical" legends, is of a supernal God, above every cosmic law, fate, and compulsion; unborn, unbegetting, knowing no desire, independent of matter and its forces; a God who does not fight other divinities or powers of impurity; who does not sacrifice, divine, prophesy, or practice sorcery; who does not sin and needs no expiation; a God who does not celebrate festivals of his life. An unfettered divine will transcending all being – that is the mark of biblical religion and that which sets it apart from all the religions of the earth.[26]

Kaufmann finds much evidence for this view in the entire *tᵉnach*, but he has to be very creative in explaining why significant prophets, among which are Hosea and Ezekiel, have warned so strongly against polytheist tendencies among the people of Israel. Put briefly, Kaufmann thinks these prophets exaggerated and actually aimed at making a different point.

Kaufmann has been criticized by many biblical and historical scholars for his claims. In an early review of his aforementioned book Philip Hyatt admits he finds himself

---

[24] Yehezkel Kaufmann, *The Religion of Israel: From its Beginnings to the Babylonian Exile*, trans. Moshe Greenberg (London: George Allen & Unwin, 1961).

[25] Kaufmann, *The Religion of Israel*, 227.   [26] Kaufmann, *The Religion of Israel*, 121.

asking many questions about Kaufmann's theories. In particular, his basic position respecting Israelite monotheism is not convincing. His view of what he calls paganism seems to me distorted, and hence his attempt to interpret the religion of Israel as utterly different and radically new fails. It appears to me to be erroneous history and inadequate theology that Hebrew religion was utterly new or unique.[27]

Comparing Vergote's position with Kaufmann's, one has to say that the former depends neither on detailed textual investigations into the history of Israel nor on the passionate drive to establish a compelling apology for Israel's unique religious identity as opposed to the religions of the world – regardless of how well one can understand this passion in Kaufmann.

However, in spite of Hyatt's harsh criticism, there is something theologically to say in favor of Kaufmann's theory, which would equally apply to Vergote. What is at stake, then, is a recognition of revelation. Whether or not there were parallels to other contemporary cultures, whether or not Moses as a historical leader of a tribe or a people was personally involved, and whether or not there was an antecedent evolution, there is something peculiar about a "moment" when a transcendent God "enters" human history to reveal Godself. Vergote and Kaufmann fundamentally acknowledge that this "moment" cannot be deduced from mere immanence and that ever since this "moment" happened, there was a community which intellectually and religiously cherished it as something to be preserved, communicated, expressed, and lived. Judaism and Christianity would be nothing without the cherishing of that unfathomable "moment" of encounter with the wholly/holy Other. In other words, biblical monotheism is a rupture in culture.

Second, there is the idea of monotheism as a critique of religion, which can be interpreted as yet another instance of how it carves in culture instead of naturally coinciding with it. Marc De Kesel, a Belgian philosopher of religion with an interest in psychoanalysis very much like Vergote, published a series of essays on monotheism in which he uses the image of the breaking of the gods.[28] A necessary consequence of a consistent monotheistic position, he observes, is that it comes with a certain intolerance toward polytheism. At best, of course, this intolerance does not manifest itself in physical violence of any kind, but it cannot be denied that, at least at an intellectual and spiritual level, there is a firmness of conviction that does not accept mixings of the one God figure with images of other deities.

---

[27] J. Philip Hyatt, "Yehezkel Kaufmann's View of the Religion of Israel," *Journal of Bible and Religion* 29 (1961) 56.

[28] Marc De Kesel, *Goden breken: Essays over monotheïsme* (Amsterdam: Boom, 2010).

According to De Kesel, monotheism is a wayward kind of religion. On the one hand, it does have rituals expressing a relationship with the supernatural as well as doctrines and confessions. All of these make it seem like any other religion.

> On the other hand, it is hard to deny that an unflinching critical attitude toward any relationship with – and belief in – the sacred, toward religion in other words, belongs without question to the mission of monotheism. To think about religion, to criticize it, to separate the wheat from the chaff, the truth from the lie, to search in every idea of God for a possible idol: it makes up the central concern and the true raison d'être of that religion.[29]

Hence, monotheism is in its very essence something ambivalent and paradoxical. It is a religion but incomparable to any "other" religion. It is a religion which revolves around "the worshiping of the truth, the true God, the divine truth. And this worship goes hand in hand – or, more radically, coincides – with the criticizing of false gods."[30] As a consequence, monotheism actively searches for such false gods so as to properly profile its own position. If it belongs to its very nature to be critical of religious beliefs, images, attitudes, and practices which do not or not sufficiently align with faith in the one and only one God, it follows, too, that ritual, social, and political systems which are based on these wrong ideas share in monotheism's criticism. Here lies, moreover, a very important foundation for the non-coincidence of the Christian religion with any political system, any nationalist ideology, and any historical regime whatsoever.[31]

According to De Kesel, who for this information relies on Jan Assmann's noted studies in Egyptology, this monotheistic religion had once popped up in Egypt with Pharaoh Ichnaton. But that cosmic form soon disappeared again. Monotheism made its entry again in the history of the people of Israel. It was refined in a more or less definitive form around the time of the Babylonian exile,[32] but took on a fundamentally different outline. Instead of being cosmically oriented, it now became political and ethical. Still in line with Assmann,

---

[29] De Kesel, *Goden breken*, 26. All translations from this book are originally mine, JG.

[30] De Kesel, *Goden breken*, 36.

[31] The consequences of this fundamental insight reach far and wide. They pertain to the relation between different peoples including their histories and self-understanding and the social, political, military, economic, and other powers bearing an influence on them. It would lead me too far astray to develop this point any further within the limits of this Element, but suffice it to say that, if and inasmuch as certain powers tend to become sacralized, and thereby unquestioned, serious questions ought to be raised in the name of Christians' faith in the one God to whom every power is (ultimately to be) subjected. Numerous examples where this necessary difference between God and deified ruling systems is nonexistent, both from the past and in the present geopolitical situation, could be given but, again, such applications would exceed the scope of this Element.

[32] De Kesel thus differs from Kaufmann in situating the historical emergence of monotheism in Israel. He relies for that on theories that are now commonly accepted among historians of religion and scholars of the Old Testament and the *tᵉnach*.

De Kesel calls this fundamental aspect the "mosaic" criterium, referring of course to Moses. He paraphrases this guideline as follows: "Nothing of what you think is God or divine, is God, only God is God."[33]

This criterium installs the critique of religion in the midst of religion itself. The core of monotheism, De Kesel argues, is *theoclastic*. "To worship the One True God consists first of all in explicitly distrusting all other gods – and everything else that presents itself as divine."[34] At the origin of every critique of ideology, De Kesel suggests, lies monotheistic religion. Whereas today it often seems as if religion and certainly institutionalized forms of Christianity are the victim of various criticisms, the very condition of possibility of those critiques may well be monotheism itself. A monotheistic image and concept of God establishes a paradigm of radical otherness and non-coincidence which is necessary to criticize any culture, thought, theory, pattern, and so on. Part of the relevance, then, of continuing to worship one God – as is done in Christian liturgies – is to not give up on a bond of confidence with the source of every possible critique of anything.

The maintenance of that relation of trust with the transcendent God is an act of faith. It manifests itself primarily in cult. Vergote's reflections on culture and religion have been helpful to further specify the Christian liturgy. It is constituted by both ritual and prayer, however with a unique monotheistic twist. That means that Christian liturgy is not only the result of a cultural development. It is also a response to God's revelation, a rupture in culture. In what follows, the question will be how the prayer-and-faith dimension of Christian liturgy expresses the belief in one true God.

2 Doxology: One God Worthy of Worship

The general answer to that question is that Christian liturgy is fundamentally doxological. In classical Greek *doxa* means opinion or reputation, but in biblical Greek the word is also used to render the idea of God's glory. In the Septuagint, the Hebrew concept of *kabod* is quite consistently translated as *doxa*. Doxology hence refers to the praising of God's glory in its different dimensions, in theology, liturgy, life, and so on. By way of preparing the next two sections of this Element, I offer a brief fundamental reflection about how doxology permeates the entire Christian liturgy and how it actually supposes a monotheistic image of God in the present one.

The focus will be first on prayer, then on theology. The two of them, however, are inextricably connected and interwoven. With Orthodox theologian Olivier Clément, who is commenting on patristic sources speaking about prayer, one

---

[33] De Kesel, *Goden breken*, 39.   [34] De Kesel, *Goden breken*, 39.

can say: "Prayer and theology are inseparable. True theology is the adoration offered by the intellect. The intellect clarifies the movement of prayer, but only prayer can give it the fervor of the Spirit. Theology is light, prayer is fire."[35] After and on the basis of these two elements, a discussion of the opposition between orthodoxy and idolatry is presented to further refine the connection between monotheism and the doxological nature of the Christian faith and religion.

2.1 Doxology and Prayer

The idea that Christian liturgy is permeated entirely by rendering praise and honor to God, that is, by worshiping Him ceaselessly, and that this implies a particular understanding of God, has been fittingly developed by the American philosopher Nicolas Wolterstorff. According to him, "[t]he deepest presupposition of the Christian liturgy is that God is worship-worthy."[36] This means that "in Christian worship we acknowledge the *unsurpassable* excellence of God."[37] Hence, liturgical prayer is fundamentally oriented toward God, who transcends the world and can never be adequately captured by the human mind. Before anything else liturgical prayer is characterized by an attitude of admiration and adoration.

Wolterstorff further unfolds what this attitude implies: awe, reverence, and gratitude. Awe corresponds to the greatness or immeasurable magnitude of God, but also to his wisdom and his continuous engagement with creation. Wolterstorff resumes:

> God's glory is manifested not only in creation but also in the incarnation, and more generally, in God's work of reconciliation of which the incarnation was the central act. The church stands in awed admiration before what I shall call God's *redemptive glory.*[38]

Corresponding with Wolterstorff's second dimension, reverence, is God's holiness. Clearly, God's holiness is a central element of many liturgical prayers. For instance, in the second Eucharistic Prayer of the Roman missal, which is based on the anaphora found in the *Traditio apostolica*,[39] God is revered for his being

---

[35] Olivier Clément, *The Roots of Christian Mysticism: Text and Commentary* (London, Dublin, and Edinburgh: New City Press, 2002), 183.

[36] Nicholas Wolterstorff, *The God We Worship: An Exploration of Liturgical Theology* (Grand Rapids and Cambridge: William B. Eerdmans, 2015), 23.

[37] Wolterstorff, *The God We Worship*, 24.   [38] Wolterstorff, *The God We Worship*, 32.

[39] This is one of the most important documents allowing insight into patterns of liturgical prayer and celebration from ancient Christianity. It was long held in scholarship that it has to be situated in Rome and that it dates from the third century CE. Its precise origins, however, are unclear and discussed by specialists. Cf. Paul F. Bradshaw, Maxwell E. Johnson, and L. Edward Philips, *The Apostolic Tradition: A Commentary* (Minneapolis: Fortress Press, 2002).

"the fount of all holiness" (*fons omnis sanctitatis*).[40] Praying can therefore be understood as asking God to share in His holiness. This implies that one also asks for the necessary strength to leave behind or overcome anything which hinders, jams, or slows down that participation.

Gratitude is the third element mentioned by Wolterstorff in his explorations of what makes God worthy of worship. This attitude of thankfulness corresponds with God's love. "Gratitude, quite obviously, is our response to God's love for us, the form of love in question being love as care, that is, love that seeks to promote the flourishing of the other and to pay due respect to her for her worth."[41] It is a bit strange that, precisely in this context, Wolterstorff does not make explicit the connection with the Eucharist as something absolutely central in the liturgical and sacramental life of Christians. Not only does the Greek word *eucharistia* itself literally means gratitude, the Eucharist has also been traditionally considered the *sacramentum caritatis*, the sacrament of love.[42]

It is not, however, because doxology permeates liturgical prayer as a whole, that one should not pay attention to other dimensions. As Wolterstorff rightly puts, "[t]he fact that the Christian liturgy as a whole is for the worship of God does not imply that no liturgical act has any purpose other than that."[43] Bearing this in mind, it makes a lot of sense to investigate what these other purposes could be, and how doxology is nevertheless related to them. A trustworthy guide for this is American liturgical theologian Don Saliers, who examined the composition of Christian liturgical prayer in admirable depth, not simply from a historical or philological point of view, but thoroughly theologically.

According to Saliers, "Christian liturgy [...] is the ongoing prayer, proclamation, and life of Jesus Christ – a sacrifice of thanksgiving and praise – offered to God in and through his body in the world. That is, Christian liturgy is our response to the self-giving of God in, with, and through the One who leads us in

---

[40] *The Roman Missal*, English translation according to the third typical edition (Collegeville: Liturgical Press, 2011), 646; OM, #100. This latter numbering of paragraphs refers to the 2008 Latin typical edition of the *Ordo Missae*, and makes it possible that different versions and editions of this liturgical document can be looked up easily.

[41] Wolterstorff, *The God We Worship*, 37.

[42] For an excellent example of that, reference can be made to Pope Benedict XVI's 2007 post-synodal apostolic exhortation "on the Eucharist as the source and the summit of the Church's life and mission" with exactly that title, *Sacramentum caritatis*. This kind of writing is published by the pope after a synod, that is, a gathering with bishops from all over the world, summarizing the most important elements that were brought forward during the consultations and discussions. The synod in question was announced under Benedict XVI's predecessor, John Paul II, who had moreover written his own last encyclical on the Eucharist (titled *Ecclesia de Eucharistia*), and took place in Rome in the autumn of 2005.

[43] Wolterstorff, *The God We Worship*, 39.

prayer."[44] As prayer, liturgy situates itself at the crossroads where God and humankind encounter each other. This means that it is always much more than the recitation of carefully drafted and selected texts, with a proper disposition abstracted from any personal involvement, but also more than the spontaneous upwelling of emotional outcries, without referring to or relying on scripted forms of prayer. In a way, through its structure, or indeed its *ordo*, liturgical prayer accommodates both more objective and more subjective ways of praying.

Analyzing patterns of liturgical prayer that have come down to us from ancient Christianity, as attested in key sources such as the *Didachè* and the *Traditio apostolica*, Saliers observes that in the whole structure of these prayers a "rhythm of praise, thanksgiving, and supplication, all mediated christologically"[45] can be seen. It is this underlying rhythm of liturgical prayer that Saliers uncovers and describes with much attention for nuance and detail.

Basically, Saliers argues, liturgical prayer consists of four constituents: (1) praising, thanking, blessing; (2) invoking and beseeching; (3) lamenting and confessing; (4) interceding. In that order. In other words, there is a certain hierarchy among these constituents, even if they tightly cohere and sometimes even overlap. The first dimension, which determines all the rest, is the doxological one. Christian liturgical prayer is uniquely characterized by rendering praise to God only, an activity which is concretized in expressing gratitude for his great saving deeds as revealed in history (the so-called *mirabilia* or *magnalia Dei*). This can only be done, however, with the assistance of God Himself, which is the reason His Holy Spirit is systematically invoked. The technical term for the invocation of the Holy Spirit is *epiclesis*.

However, all of this remains in vain or risks becoming meaningless, if the truth about human beings' deepest drives and motivations is not made explicit. True prayer supposes a purity of heart, a firmness of conviction, as well as an honest awareness that not everything always goes well. In other words, lament and confession are necessary aspects of liturgical prayer, as is the connection with the world and the needs of the people inhabiting it. Christians in their liturgies have the duty to remember the actual and real state of the world when they gather. "Intercession is a fundamental vocation of the church. It shows kinship with lamentation. We are to pray for the world in all its suffering. But this requires looking clearly and honestly at the world and at ourselves as we really are."[46]

---

[44] Don E. Saliers, *Worship as Theology: Foretaste of Glory Divine* (Nashville: Abingdon Press, 1994), 86.
[45] Saliers, *Worship as Theology*, 95.   [46] Saliers, *Worship as Theology*, 126.

It is worth quoting Saliers at some length to hear how he conceives of the coherence of the first two dimensions of liturgical prayer, and thus to hear how he presents its doxological and epicletic nature.

> Christian liturgy is, first and last, praising, blessing, and thanking God. It is a continual speaking of God's name in gratitude and thankfulness for the self-giving of God to the world. On occasion it sings ecstatic praise for the very *being* of the source of all creation: *Te deum laudamus*. Yet every liturgical assembly, as every prayer in the name of Jesus, is radically dependent upon the gift of God's presence. Therefore all true worship begins and ends with a calling upon the name of the triune God, whose Holy Spirit gives life to our worship. This praying to God gives evidence to both absence and presence, and no human act in and of itself can overcome the gap between the experienced absence or distance from God and the divine presence. So we begin again and again by invoking the name and Spirit of God.[47]

Interestingly, neither Wolterstorff nor Saliers explicitly deals with the question of monotheism in their explorations of the doxological nature of Christian liturgical prayer. Yet it seems so evident for them that God is one, unique, and universal, that alternatives to a monotheistic image of God simply do not occur to them. As such they are representative of many philosophers and theologians investigating the worship and prayer of Christians. Monotheism, therefore, seems to be an axiom of liturgical prayer. None of it works or fits if that is not taken for granted.

2.2 Doxology and Theology

In addition to giving shape to the nature of liturgical prayer, doxology is also said to determine the ultimate purpose of theology. The goal of doing theology thus lies not only in shedding light on intellectual difficulties sprouting forth from the fact that people respond in faith to God revealing Himself, but also, in and through that work of the intellect, in rendering homage to the One from where everything seems to have started and to which everything returns. It needs to be added, however, that this doxological dimension underlying theology as a whole has for a very long time been neglected and obscured, that it was sometimes fully forgotten, and that is was even put aside as a naïve form of piety.

It is likely that an underestimation of the doxological *archè* and *telos* of theology – that is, its origin and its end, and therefore its guiding principle – is still common today. Not many academic theologians would say straightforwardly and with ease that theology's actual and ultimate aim is to glorify God as the one and only. They would refrain from such a grotesque claim and rather

---

[47] Saliers, *Worship as Theology*, 118.

frame theology's goals in more modest, graspable, and secular terms. It seems indeed difficult to be clear about (academic) theology's doxological orientation in public fora.

According to Kevin Irwin, the rediscovery of theology's fundamental doxological core and outline had to do predominantly with the growing influence of the study of ancient Christian sources, as was the case exemplarily among proponents of the *nouvelle théologie* and the Liturgical Movement, who were active in redesigning the field of theology around the middle of the twentieth century. In the introduction to his pioneering and influential monograph on Eucharistic prayers, Louis Bouyer draws his readers' attention to

> the theology which was latent in the ancient eucharist. Obviously what we have here is a theology with which our modern manuals have not familiarized us – and this is surely why its discovery can be so delightful! This theology, as exacting as it may be (and it is in its own way), remains very close to the first meaning of the Greek θεολογια, which designates a hymn, a glorification of God by the λογος, man's expressed thought.[48]

Irwin underscores the particular importance of these thoughts for liturgical theology. In that context he moreover refers to the work of American Catholic theologian Catherine LaCugna, who wrote a groundbreaking study on Trinitarian theology and sadly died much too early. Irwin notes that for LaCugna liturgy and theology are intrinsically related because of an "inner moment" shared by both, namely doxology. Liturgy is "a *mysterium salutis* that unites soteriology and doxology."[49] Consequently, she continues, with a wink to Bonaventure, "it is proper to describe theology not as the *itinerarium mentis in Deum* but the *itinerarium in mysterium salutis*, and therefore, the *itinerarium doxologicum*."[50] With these concepts LaCugna reorients the course of theology from a focus on the mind's journey into God toward a focus on a journey into the mystery of salvation. That journey, she says, is fundamentally a doxological journey.

It goes without saying that this means a significant broadening and deepening of the theological enterprise. LaCugna's emphatic rephrasing of Bonaventure's understanding of theology means that much more than the thinking and cognitive faculties of the human person is involved. In addition to something

---

[48] Louis Bouyer, *Eucharist: Theology and Spirituality of the Eucharistic Prayer*, trans. Charles Underhill Quinn (Notre Dame: University of Notre Dame Press, 2006 [1968]), 5; cf. Kevin W. Irwin, *Context and Text: A Method for Liturgical Theology*, rev. ed. (Collegeville: Liturgical Press, 2018), 508.

[49] Irwin, *Context and Text*, 510.

[50] Catherine Mowry LaCugna, "Can Liturgy Ever Again Be a Source for Theology," *Studia Liturgica* 19 (1989) 13. Quoted – but incorrectly referenced – in Irwin, *Context and Text*, 511.

epistemological, theology becomes something communal as well as existential if its nature is redefined in terms of soteriology and doxology.[51] It is not only about helping one's reflections reach toward the divine, but about a full participation in the economy of salvation.

Underlying LaCugna's profound conviction that *theologia* and *oikonomia* are fundamentally about one and the same comprehensive reality, God's life and love, is Karl Rahner's renowned dictum about the identity of the immanent and economic trinity or, put in simpler terms, God's inner being and God's acting outward. LaCugna somehow radicalized Rahner's idea that one cannot separate the life of God in and out of Himself from the ways in which He, being Father, Son, and Spirit, is engaged in human history.[52] All of these are centered around communion. God's innermost being is love-in-communion, as much as communion-in-love constitutes the deepest vocation of humankind and the highest call of Christian faith. Theology is there to investigate the many dimensions of "communion" with God's glory, and as such cannot but be totally steeped in doxology.

This vision has been systematically developed by the British Methodist theologian and noted ecumenist Geoffrey Wainwright. His personal vision, he says, "is firmly shaped and strongly coloured by the Christian liturgy."[53] Liturgy is the place par excellence where the vision is expressed, where people live it, and where it can also be transmitted. "Into the liturgy the people bring their entire existence so that it may be gathered up in praise. From the liturgy the people depart with a renewed vision of the value-patterns of God's kingdom, by the more effective practice of which they intend to glorify God in their whole life."[54] Doctrines and theologies help elucidate what all of this means.

For Wainwright, whose work is known and greatly valued by LaCugna, the real connection theology needs to have with life, liturgy, and doctrine is crucial. All of them are permeated by a profound doxological orientation.

> I see Christian worship, doctrine and life as conjoined in a common "upwards" and "forwards" direction towards God and the achievement of his purpose, which includes human salvation. They intend God's praise. His glory is that he is already present and within to enable our transformation into his likeness, which means participation in himself and his kingdom.[55]

---

[51] At this point it makes sense to signal a profound congruence between LaCugna and Vagaggini (cf. p. 9 above).

[52] Catherine Mowry LaCugna, *God for Us: The Trinity and Christian Life* (San Francisco: Harper Collins, 1991), 211–217, 224.

[53] Geoffrey Wainwright, *Doxology: The Praise of God in Worship, Doctrine, and Life: A Systematic Theology* (New York: Oxford University Press, 1980), 1.

[54] Wainwright, *Doxology*, 8.   [55] Wainwright, *Doxology*, 10.

Again, as was the case with prayer, the notion of participation appears to be central. Theology's aim is to explain how the contents of faith, the practices of Christians and, above anything else yet intimately related with everything, their liturgies contribute to rendering veritable praise to God. The many and diverse ways in which God's *doxa* is manifested, expressed and lived in historical circumstances are, and should be, theology's ultimate focus. This cannot be thought of otherwise than by supposing a reality which God and humankind can share.

The sharing of this reality is best conceived of as a dynamic, not as a static situation or a mere immovable sphere. Both Wainwright and LaCugna conceive of the divine doxa in which humans are invited to participate and with which they can to some extent cooperate in a dynamic way. Rather implicitly than explicitly, like Wolterstorff and Saliers, they also adhere to a pure Christian monotheism. This equals for them a Trinitarian theology, one God, considered Father, Son, and Holy Spirit, whose presence is an activating agency realizing a deep transformation of the human lifeworld.

2.3 Doxology, Orthodoxy, and Idolatry

However, the human collaboration with that divinely initiated transformation can go massively and terribly wrong. The danger that the human partner in the relationship puts themselves at the level of the divine is always lurking. The praise of God can always become the praise of oneself. However, without transcendence or without an absolute other on the other side of the relationship, the act of praising makes itself undone. Doxology doesn't work if there is no radical otherness. Hence, it does not come as a surprise that the notion of orthodoxy enters the scene.

It is important to rightly understand the concept of orthodoxy. Aidan Kavanagh's noted clarification is most helpful in that respect. Orthodoxy, he explains, has been too often identified "as 'correct doctrine' to be maintained by centralized ecclesiastical authority having exclusive power to enforce an absolute standard in liturgical texts by law."[56] As a reaction to this mentality, Kavanagh simply puts forward that orthodoxy "means first 'right worship' and only secondarily doctrinal accuracy."[57] This anchoring of theology in liturgy is essential for him; it must lead to "a life of 'right worship' which quite overflows what goes on in churches during divine service to permeate all aspects of a faithful community's daily business."[58] Orthodoxy is there, primarily and ultimately, to sustain and to orient the worship of believers. If that means

---

[56] Kavanagh, *On Liturgical Theology*, 81.   [57] Kavanagh, *On Liturgical Theology*, 3.
[58] Kavanagh, *On Liturgical Theology*, 177.

that precise formulations of faith contents have to be developed, then that must be done, but it can never be done if one loses out of sight the real goal.

Saliers concurs with this insight and, like Kavanagh, makes allusions to the etymological meaning of the word orthodoxy. He moreover brings in the issue of monotheism.

> *Ortho-doxa* means right praise to God. *Doxa*, of course, has the wonderful ambiguity of referring both to human belief and to something intrinsic to God: doxa as the divine glory. *Ortho-doxa* is the practice of right ascription of honor and praise and glory to the One to whom all such ascription is due. [. . .] *Orthodoxy*, then, in the first instance, returns to the very font [. . .] of this God of glory. *Orthodoxy* is learning in the long, hard, joyous way to ascribe unto God the *doxa* due God's name.[59]

Situating the roots of orthodoxy in doxology makes one additionally understand that the opposite of orthodoxy is actually not heterodoxy, in the sense of erroneous thinking or upholding false ideas. Instead the opposite of orthodoxy is idolatry. Not acting in an orthodox way is much less about having deviant opinions than that it is about worshiping wrong gods. As a consequence, idolatry is rather in the order of doing than in the order of thinking.

Orthodoxy and also, consequently, idolatry are profoundly liturgical notions before they turn over into matters of theological epistemology and criteriology. Not being orthodox is worshiping what is not worthy of worship. Idolatry is shifting the focus from the one and only God worthy of worship to other things, usually created ones. It is setting the wrong priorities in liturgy and prayer and thereby subjecting oneself to things unworthy of worship.

This is a matter of paramount existential importance in Christian faith and for the Christian Church. As a community and as an individual person it is crucial to keep oneself focused on God in worship and prayer and to avoid situations where one actually worships wrongly or unworthy things. In practice, this seems by no means evident. Wainwright pointedly explains how idolatry happens:

> The making of humanity in the divine image means that humanity has the potential to reveal God. That capacity will be realized when, through communion with God in response to the divine vocation, human beings grow into his existential and moral "likeness". But the making of humanity in the divine image was also dangerous. It gives human beings the opportunity to mistake *themselves* for God. The distinction between Creator and creature is then left out of consideration. Instead of being gratefully received as a gift, the human similarity to God is asserted as a right. That is the meaning of the *temptation*, "You shall be like God" (Genesis 3:5). The potential for creativity which

---
[59] Saliers, *Worship as Theology*, 40–41.

humanity derives from God becomes devoted to the manufacture of idols. [...] Idols are in the last resort a form of human self-worship: *I* give value to what *I* choose.[60]

As a consequence, orthodox Christian liturgies always rest on a breaking of the idols of the world and/or on a rupture within the circle of the self so that it can orient itself toward transcendence.[61] They are designed in such a way that all the worship is directed to God only, and that all human activity is transformed toward that goal.

Someone like German theologian and New Testament scholar Gerhard Lohfink very sharply realizes that this is not at all obvious. At the outset of a recent book he published on Christian prayer, he presents the probable results of an imagined examination of a representative sample of Christians when they are asked to whom they actually pray.

> I am convinced that a large percentage of those questioned would say: "God, of course. Who else?" – and that answer would be theologically wrong. Why? Because Christians do not pray to God; they pray either to God the Father or to Jesus Christ or to the Holy Spirit. Of course they believe in the *one* God and confess, with Israel, that there is but *one* God, but whenever they are praying to this God they address themselves to the Father, the Son, or the Holy Spirit.[62]

Clearly, Lohfink problematizes here the relationship between monotheism and belief in the Trinity. He gives voice to the fact that it is not evident to combine the two. That is not only the case at an intellectual theological level, but also liturgically. Avoiding idolatry, focusing on the right object of worship – that is, God only, and only one God – and entertaining orthodoxy through the right use of doxologies is, has always been, and will always be a challenge for Christians. It is the liturgical wager of Christianity. However, not betting is not an option. Not betting is always losing, and being lost.

To be sure, while realizing how extraordinary it is, Lohfink strongly defends the Trinitarian monotheism of the Christian faith.

> Christians do not worship three gods! They explicitly confess faith in the *one* God, the God of Abraham, Isaac, and Jacob. Worship of the triune God does *not* mean that there are three gods; rather, it says that all honor, all worship, all praise belongs to God the Father. But at the same time worship of the triune God affirms that ultimately the Father can only be known and glorified through the Son and in the Holy Spirit.[63]

---

[60] Wainwright, *Doxology*, 34–35.

[61] This ties in of course with what was said above with reference to De Kesel and Vergote.

[62] Gerhard Lohfink, *Prayer Takes Us Home: The Theology and Practice of Christian Prayer*, trans. Linda M. Maloney (Collegeville: Liturgical Press, 2020), 1.

[63] Lohfink, *Prayer Takes Us Home*, 16.

It is an immense challenge to show how the "at the same time" in the above quote actually works. The conviction that, together with – that is, without making any distinctions or giving in to subordinating schemes – God the Father's being worthy of worship, as the one true God, is set forth in the worshiping of God the Son, Jesus Christ, as well as in the worshiping of the Holy Spirit, requires a lot of explanation. It means that an examination in some detail of traditional liturgical material is now at stake.

3 Doxologies: A Survey of Traditional Liturgical Material

The aim of the present section is to investigate some textual liturgical material from the Christian tradition which can give us a better insight into how doxological formulae express Christians' faith in one God. In other words, a representative sample of liturgical texts from the Christian tradition will be presented in order to see and evaluate how monotheism is manifested in them. The hypothesis undergirding this presentation of liturgical material is that the doxologies have a distinctive Trinitarian character.

In the technical jargon of liturgical studies, a doxology is a prayer or part of a prayer in which God's praise – and nothing else – is expressed. Doxologies are found everywhere in the liturgy, but above all in the Eucharist and in the liturgy of the hours. The Eucharist and the liturgy of the hours beautifully illustrate the liturgy's nature as both ritual and prayer. These two basic regimes of Christian liturgy, though in different proportions, can be said to fundamentally consist of a series of ritualized prayers. A central concern in the process of ritualizing has always been to assure that the right order of worship is respected. Put differently, the prayers had to be orthodox, meaning that the doxologies expressed in and through them are the right ones.

According to LaCugna, the roots of orthodoxy in doxology are a historical reality. She traces the origins of what became standard Trinitarian monotheism in ancient Christian debates over the position of Christ, the Son of God, and the Holy Spirit, toward God the Father. Different traditions in liturgical practice had developed, and they left an indelible mark on further evolutions in Trinitarian theology. Crucial in this development was the stance of the Cappadocians, that is, the common name for three influential Church fathers of the fourth century, Basil the Great, his brother Gregory of Nyssa, and their close friend Gregory of Nazianzus. The Cappadocians' theologies have been instrumental in reconciling biblical monotheism with a Trinitarian understanding of God and the economy of salvation. "For Basil," LaCugna explains, "as for all orthodox theologians to follow, it was of utmost importance to show that to worship the

God of Jesus Christ in the traditional doxology was the same as to worship God *as such*, in whom there is neither subordination nor inequality of persons."[64]

It is this pattern that will guide us in the investigations of liturgical material below. The leading questions are: How is the worship of God equal to the worship of Jesus Christ? How are the figure of the Father and the figure of the Son related in liturgical sources that have given shape to and continue to determine Christian liturgy? And what can these sources hence teach us in terms of monotheism? Also, are things as radical as Lohfink suggests? Is it theologically "wrong" to address liturgical prayer to God instead of to the Father, the Son, or the Holy Spirit? To be sure, less attention will be paid below to the specific role the Holy Spirit plays. This would substantially expand the scope of this Element, and within these confines it is not necessary theologically to discuss in detail how the doctrine of the Spirit fits in the whole.[65] A lot which will be said about the Father and the Son applies mutatis mutandis to the Holy Spirit.

The present section consists of three parts. First, psalms and hymns will be discussed. They have constituted Christian liturgical prayer for centuries. So it seems a good move to start there to see how they are expressive of a Christian Trinitarian monotheism.

Second, two *psalmi idiotici* are highlighted. The term *psalmi idiotici* refers to discussions in early Christianity, when in addition to psalms from the Bible many other psalm-like prayers, hymns, were composed and taken up in worship services. At a certain point the Church's leadership reacted against these "self-made" or indeed "idiotic" psalms and forbade their use in the liturgy. Some, however, whose orthodoxy was guaranteed, were kept and thereupon exerted an immeasurable influence on the liturgy. Among these are the *Gloria in excelsis Deo* and the *Te Deum laudamus*, which still have a prominent role in the celebration of the Eucharist and the liturgy of the hours. On close inspection, these two prayers reveal a great deal about how the worship of God the Father is extended to, and actually not different from, the worship of Jesus Christ.

Third, it is essential to have a look as well at the anaphoras or Eucharistic prayers, which constitute the core of the Eucharistic celebration in different liturgical and ecclesial traditions. Apparently, care has been taken to have these prayers start and end with fitting doxologies. If and inasmuch as it is true that

---

[64] LaCugna, *God for Us*, 121.

[65] Having said this, it is not unimportant to mention that, according to many scholars throughout the twentieth century, there has been a significant forgetfulness or even neglect of the Holy Spirit in the history of Western theologies. This analysis has often given rise to critical considerations and to proposals for renewal. Exemplary in this respect is Yves Congar 's masterly study *Je crois en l'Esprit Saint* (Paris: Cerf, 1997).

Christian prayer finds its highest expression in the Eucharist, and thus that it is set within and permeated by doxology, as Saliers asserts, the Eucharistic prayer cannot but be a, if not the, most adequate illustration of this.

3.1 Psalms, Canticles, and Hymns as Christian Liturgical Prayers

The history and composition of the liturgy of the hours in different liturgical and ecclesial traditions is a very complex subject.[66] Basically, the liturgy of the hours or divine office consists of psalms, hymns, readings from the Bible, as well as petitions or intercessions for the needs of the world. The proportions and distribution of this and indeed some other material over the individual hours in the course of a day, a week, and a year vary in different liturgical rites or families. But the idea is that all the individual elements together are supportive of "the real aim" of daily prayer, which is "unbroken communion with God."[67] This communion, moreover, is imagined as a sharing in God's glory. The whole liturgy of the hours is regarded as a glorification of God and, in and through that, a sanctification of time and world. Or, in LaCugna's vocabulary, the liturgy of the hours reflects both *theologia* and *oikonomia*.

Traditionally, monasticism has determined the shape of the liturgy of the hours to a great extent. One of its distinctive characteristics was the continuous recitation of the psalms, that is, the 150 psalms from the book of the same name in the Bible. The first Christians had moreover developed an encompassing Christological interpretation of the psalms, which made them say that the psalms actually speak of Christ, or to Christ, or that Christ in one way or another speaks through them.[68] Bradshaw expresses himself critically about this Christological interpretation and submits that it relies on "an understanding of prophecy and its fulfillment [which] does not easily accord with that commonly held today," whence "it is hardly surprising that the recitation of psalms has been found to present considerable difficulties for contemporary Christian worship."[69] In spite of these difficulties, however, it is still the case that the psalms, interpreted Christologically, constitute a core element of the liturgy of the hours in the Roman rite.

---

[66] Paul F. Bradshaw, *Daily Prayer in the Early Church: A Study of the Origin and Early Development of the Divine Office* (London: SPCK, 1981); Robert Taft, *The Liturgy of the Hours in East and West: The Origins of the Divine Office and its Meaning for Today*, 2nd rev. ed. (Collegeville: Liturgical Press, 1993).

[67] Bradshaw, *Daily Prayer*, 151.

[68] Balthasar Fischer, "Le Christ dans les psaumes: La dévotion aux psaumes dans l'Église des martyrs," *La Maison-Dieu* 27 (1951) 86–113. In spite of its age, Fischer's article, which resumes the major conclusions of his doctoral dissertation, still counts as authoritative for this specific subject matter.

[69] Bradshaw, *Daily Prayer*, 152.

The psalms themselves are regarded as prayers of praise, and thus profoundly doxological. In the General Instruction of the Liturgy of the Hours, the Catholic Church holds:

> "The psalms are not readings or prose prayers, but poems of praise. They can on occasion be recited as readings, but from their literary genre they are properly called *Tehillim* ('songs of praise') in Hebrew and *psalmoi* ('songs to be sung to the lyre') in Greek. In fact, all the psalms have a musical quality that determines their correct style of delivery."[70]

This automatic coupling of the psalms' doxological nature with their musicality is not a mere detail. It underscores the idea that Christian worship is a collaborative action before it is expressed more coherently in thoughts and principles.

The making of psalms into Christian prayer par excellence has found a noteworthy expression in the fact that praying them has been accompanied by systematically adding a doxological formula (Table 1). This addition was common practice already in the fourth century CE, even if the exact phrasing of it differed from the one that has become the most frequently used. In Table 1 the standard Latin wording and a common English translation are shown.

Table 1 The doxology after the psalms

Latin text	**English translation**
Gloria Patri et Filio et Spiritui Sancto.	Glory be to the Father, and to the Son, and to the Holy Spirit.
Sicut erat in principio et nunc et semper et in saecula saeculorum. Amen.	As it was in the beginning, is now, and ever shall be, world without end. Amen.

What strikes one in these simple lines is the perfect equality of praise of the Father, the Son, and the Holy Spirit as expressed in the conjunction "and" (*et*). The glory that is due to the Father is the same as the one that is due to the Son and the Spirit. This is further specified by the second line, in the sense that this is and should be the case eternally. In other words, no distinction is made, nor can there ever be made a division, between the three persons of the Trinity as far as praise to them is concerned. Both in the first line starting with *Gloria*, thus expressing the program of everything which follows, and in the second line starting with *Sicut erat*, the doxological content manifests a firm monotheism: *one* form of praise for the Trinity in *all* times.

---

[70] *General Instruction of the Liturgy of the Hours*, #103. As quoted in *The Liturgy Documents: A Parish Resource*, vol. 2 (Chicago: Liturgy Training Publications, 1999), 287.

It seems that this doxological embedding of the psalms in the liturgy of the hours sheds an important light on their being interpreted Christologically. As Matthieu Collin, biblical scholar and monk, underscores, a Christological interpretation of the psalms is not an improper supplement of meaning showing little respect for their original context. It has nothing whatsoever to do with supersessionism. Collin sees in the psalms the cries and the jubilation of humankind in its ongoing dialogue with God. And it is precisely in *all* the aspects of human experience and life that Jesus Christ can be discovered. Christ is revealed in the psalms *in* the thickness of the biblical tissue,[71] not on top of it. The psalms express the full breadth and depth of human experience and the vicissitudes of life.

Interestingly, the book of psalms closes with a series of psalms of praise or laudatory psalms. The literary unit of psalms 145–150 could be considered as one extended doxology, in which not only humanity but the entire creation is involved.[72] At the end of psalm 145 the program of the five following psalms is announced: "My mouth will speak the praise of the LORD, and all flesh will bless his holy name forever and ever" (Ps 145:21). Correspondingly, the next five psalms each open *and* close with the word *Hallelujah*, which literally means "praise the Lord" (Ps 146:1.10; 147:1.20; 148:1.14; 149:1.9; 150:1.6).

The liturgical tradition of the Roman rite has been profoundly aware of the uniqueness of this literary unit. It has preserved the praying of these psalms for special moments and connected them in particular with the "hinges" of the liturgy of the hours, that is, lauds and vespers. Every transition from light to darkness in the evening and from the darkness of the night to the morning light are fitting occasions to sing God's praises and to remember his works.

In addition to the psalms, the Church has known a tradition to select other texts from Scripture and insert them into her official liturgical prayer. The technical term for these biblical prayers not from the book of psalms is canticles. At present, the Roman rite has no less than twenty-six such canticles from the Old Testament as part of its psalmody for the hour of lauds. The majority among them are taken from the book of Isaiah, but there are also excerpts from Tobit, Judith, Habakkuk, and Jeremiah, as well as the song of Hannah from 1 Samuel 2 (1–10), some lines of which intriguingly resonate in the Magnificat,[73] and the

---

[71] Matthieu Collin, *Comme un murmure de cithare: Introduction aux Psaumes* (Paris and Perpignan: Desclée de Brouwer, 2007), 282.

[72] Collin, *Comme un murmure*, 155–166.

[73] There are three evangelic canticles, canticles that are taken from the gospel (in all cases the gospel of Luke): the *Magnificat* or Song of Mary at vespers (Lk 1:46–55), the *Benedictus* or Song of Zechariah at lauds (Lk 1:68–79), and the *Nunc dimittis* or Song of Simeon at compline (Lk 2:29–32). All three of them are considered as songs of praise par excellence.

song of Moses from Deuteronomy 32 (1–12). The most famous among these Old Testament canticles, however, is probably the song of the three youths or three children from Daniel 3. The so-called *canticum trium puerorum* has marked morning prayer on Sundays for centuries.[74] Through an intriguing enumeration of the different elements of which the cosmos consists, including meteorological phenomena and vegetative and animal life, the text evokes how the entire creation is involved in singing the Creator's praises. The interesting point here is that all of these biblical texts are made into Christian liturgical prayer in the same way as the psalms, that is, by letting them culminate in exactly the same Trinitarian doxology.

Apart from Old Testament canticles, the liturgy of the hours of the Roman rite now also includes canticles from the New Testament (Table 2). This was a consequence of the liturgical reforms issuing forth from the Second Vatican Council in the late 1960s. Of course this helps one realize what it means that the Church always prays with Christ, through Christ, and to Christ. The distribution of the New Testament canticles over the seven days of the week in evening prayer is as follows.[75]

Table 2 New Testament canticles in the vespers of the Roman rite

Days of the week	New Testament canticle
Saturday (vespers I of Sunday)	Philippians 2:6–11
Sunday (vespers II)	Revelation 19:1–2.5–7 *or* 1 Peter 2:21–24 in lent
Monday	Ephesians 1:3–10
Tuesday	Revelation 4:11; 5:9.10.12
Wednesday	Colossians 1:12–20
Thursday	Revelation 11:17–18; 12:10b–12a
Friday	Revelation 15:3–4

---

[74] The current situation in the *Liturgia horarum* of the Roman rite is that this song is split into two. In the four-week distribution of psalmody, verses 57–88 plus verse 56 from Daniel 3 are scheduled on Sundays I and III; verses 52–57 are sung on Sundays II and IV. This redistribution of psalms and canticles over a period of four weeks was a novelty of the liturgical reforms in the wake of Vatican II. Previously, the entire psalter was spread over one week only, as was the case in the *Regula* of Benedict of Nursia.

[75] The Old Testament canticles are part of lauds, the New Testament canticles of vespers. This ordering expresses the movement from the history of salvation toward the figure of Christ, always to be repeated and renewed. The psalmody part of both lauds and vespers consists of three psalms, two of which are taken from the psalter (it is also possible that one longer psalm is subdivided into two parts) and one of which is thus a canticle. In lauds, the canticle comes second; in vespers it occupies the third place.

Most of the New Testament canticles in the vespers of the Roman rite are taken from the book of Revelation.[76] All of them embody the idea that praise is due to God, but particularly noteworthy is the canticle taken from Revelation 15, as it is based on the "song of the Lamb" in the context of which an emphatic monotheistic theme comes to the fore:

> Great and amazing are your deeds,
>   Lord God the Almighty!
> Just and true are your ways,
>   King of the nations!
> Lord, who will not fear
>   and glorify your name?
> For you alone are holy.
>   All nations will come
>   and worship before you,
> for your judgments have been revealed.
>
>   (Rev 15:3–4 NRSV)

The idea that God alone is holy and that this is what makes him the only one worthy of worship is representative of the liturgy as a whole. The verse where this is said in so many words (Rev 15:4) has borne an immense impact on liturgical prayer.

All the other New Testament canticles are taken from the Pauline corpus. Here it is the Christ hymn of Philippians 2, sung every Saturday night and on the eve of major feasts, which deserves special mention. This famous hymn with its two stanzas, the one expressing Christ's kenosis or self-emptying and his taking-on of the form of a slave, and the other one contrasting this lowering with Jesus' divine exaltation, culminates in the call that

> every tongue should confess
> that Jesus Christ is Lord,
> to the glory of God the Father.
>
>   (Phil 2:11 NRSV)

Again, this one single and simple verse entails in a nutshell what the entire Christian worship revolves around. It is built around the conviction that God's glory is extended, expressed, and exemplified in the confession that Jesus Christ

---

[76] In this context is not uninteresting to mention that in the book of Revelation a series of early Christian liturgical material was integrated. The famous Lutheran theologian, exegete, and ecumenist Oscar Cullmann noted in his much acclaimed study *Urchristentum und Gottesdienst*: "The familiar songs of the early Christian service which are preserved for us again in the Johannine Apocalypse are partly of direct Jewish descent and partly modelled on the Jewish songs. We may mention here the following as the oldest of all Christian songs: Rev. 5.9; 5.12; 12.10-12; 19.1-2; 19.6." Oscar Cullmann, *Early Christian Worship*, trans. A. Stewart Todd and James B. Torrance (London: SCM Press, 1969 [1953]), 21.

is the Lord. The mysteries of Jesus Christ are the culmination point of God's revelation and therefore constitutive of the liturgy. The confession of Jesus' lordship, understood as not different either in degree or in quality from God's own lordship, uniquely characterizes the Christian liturgy.

In a thorough and classical study on Christian liturgical prayer, James Crichton explained how, on the one hand, God's otherness and transcendence was preserved in the primitive Church, among other things to avoid pantheism, and how, on the other hand, God's incarnation in Christ gave a clearer focus to the "intimations of the Immanuel" of which the Old Testament testifies. This convergence of transcendence and concretization was and is essential for Christian liturgical prayer. It accounts for Christians' use of the psalms and – one could add – of the canticles from both the Old and the New Testament "with confidence and without *arrière-pensée*." "This development was no doubt assisted by the translation of Yahweh in the psalms by the word '*Kyrios*' which the New Testament applied to Christ without hesitation."[77] Further on, we will see how the interlocking of the honor due to God and that due to Christ is the key to other elements of Christian liturgy as well.

In addition to psalms and canticles, the liturgy of the hours in the Roman rite also consists of hymns. Some of them have very old origins and are attributed to famous personalities such as the fourth-century Church father Ambrose of Milan or Gregory the Great, who was the pope at the end of the sixth century. Hymns open the individual hours and set the tone for the celebration. Many hymns are particularly reserved for a solemnity, an octave or a season, or indeed an hour. They help the community direct their thoughts to what it is that they are celebrating. Usually they have, or at least have had, a distinctive melody of their own. Singing them differs from the singing of the psalms. The balance between text and music is different. Often they excel in literary quality, as they have rhyme and rhythm when pronounced in the Latin original. As such they significantly differ from the psalms, which, as Hebrew poetry, display a completely different poetic system and accordingly obey other literary standards.

What matters, however, in the context of this Element is neither their musicality nor their rich contents and poetical expressiveness, but the fact that all of them end with Trinitarian formulae in which at the same time a Christian monotheism is expressed. In other words, the treasure of the Latin hymns of the Church is an important locus where an extraordinary variety of Trinitarian *and* monotheistic ideas can be found. The theological cement between all these portions of texts is, unsurprisingly, doxology.

---

[77] Crichton, *Christian Celebration*, 81.

It would lead us too far astray to even try to study a representative sample of the hymn endings in detail, but a selection of a few well-chosen examples is certainly in order. In the context of matins, lauds, and vespers of the paschal triduum two famous hymns, which were probably composed by Venantius Fortunatus (late sixth century, Gaul), are used: *Pange, lingua, gloriosi (lauream certaminis)*, and *Vexilla regis prodeunt*, respectively. The first one ends as follows:[78]

Sempiterna sit beatae	Eternal honor be unto you
Trinitati gloria,	Holy Trinity
Aequa Patri, Filioque;	In like manner to the Father and the Son;
Par decus Paraclito:	Equal homage to the Paraclete:
Unius Trinique nomen	The name of the one and three
Laudet universitas. Amen.	Let the whole cosmos praise. Amen.

The ending of the second one is more straightforwardly Trinitarian and less strictly monotheistic:

Te, fons salutis, Trinitas,	You, source of salvation, Trinity,
Collaudet omnis spiritus:	Should praise every mind:
Quibus Crucis victoriam	To whom the victory of the Cross
Largiris, adde praemium. Amen	You bestowed, add a reward. Amen

In a contemporary book of the hours, the Benedictine Daily Prayer book edited by the outstanding liturgical scholar and oblate of Saint John's Abbey in Minnesota, Maxwell Johnson, all the Trinitarian endings of the hours of the paschal triduum, based on the abovementioned ancient hymns, are nevertheless the same:

> To the Father, Son, and Spirit,
> Equal praise be given now,
> As we call to mind Christ's Passion,
> And in deep repentance bow. Amen.[79]

When he was composing the liturgical material for the solemnity of Corpus Christi, newly established for the universal Church by pope Urban IV in 1264,

---

[78] All translations into English of the Latin original of the subsequent texts are mine, JG. I opted for literal translations that stay as close as possible to the Latin text. More poetic translations and versions used in the liturgy of the hours can obviously be found in liturgical books and on websites.

[79] *Benedictine Daily Prayer: A Short Breviary*, compiled and ed. Maxwell E. Johnson (Dublin: The Columba Press, 2005), 1501, 1507, 1513, 1515. These references are taken from Holy Friday, but the use of this Trinitarian ending of the hymns of the week before Easter is of course much broader.

Thomas Aquinas made use of Venantius Fortunatus' well-worn opening lines. In so doing, Aquinas made an interesting theological connection between the Feast of the Body and Blood of Christ and the Lord's passion as it is remembered and celebrated in the context of Good Friday.[80] Still in use for the first and second vespers of the feast of Corpus Christi, Aquinas' hymn *Pange lingua gloriosi (corporis mysterium)*, which became more famous than the hymn to which its opening lines refers, ends with the following stanza:

Genitori, Genitoque	To the Procreator and the Begotten one
Laus et iubilatio,	Let there be praise and jubilation,
Salus, honor, virtus quoque,	Salvation, honor and also virtue,
Sit et benedictio:	as well as blessing:
Procendenti ab utroque	And to the one who came forth from both
Compar sit laudatio. Amen.	Let there be equal praise.

This, granted, all too brief sample of Trinitarian endings of hymns used in the liturgy of the hours of the Roman rite corroborates the overall doxological orientation of all liturgical prayer. In and through this constitutive portion of the psalms, the canticles and the hymns in the liturgy of the hours elements of a Christian monotheism beautifully shine through. The prevailing idea is that only the Trinity is worthy of worship: Father, Son, and Holy Spirit are met with equal and the same praise.

3.2 Two *psalmi idiotici*

As the worship of Christians in the early Church continued to develop, more and more material found its way to the different services and celebrations. The closeness to Scripture was usually obvious but, as time went by, a new genre emerged. It was characterized by an imitation of biblical poetry, especially the psalms, but drew on material from other biblical books as well. The Council of Laodicea, which gathered in the early 60s of the fourth century, called these texts *psalmi idiotici*, because they were self-made and not copied from Scripture. It strictly reduced their number, for it was concerned that too much lyrical freedom would easily give rise to unorthodox prayer. In other words, the Council was concerned about doxology and/as right worship. Nevertheless, its canons permitted the use of a small selection of *psalmi idiotici* including the *Gloria in excelsis Deo* and the *Te Deum laudamus*,

---

[80] For a remarkable commentary on Aquinas' Eucharistic poetry, see Jan-Heiner Tück, *Gabe der Gegenwart: Theologie und Dichtung der Eucharistie bei Thomas von Aquin* (Freiburg, Basel, and Wien: Herder, 2009). Tück argues that there is large theological correspondence between Aquinas' theoretical speculations about the Eucharist and the hymnic and devotional material he wrote for the feast of Corpus Christi.

which are still in use today. An attentive reading of these two texts unveils a lot about Christian monotheism as embodied by the Church's liturgical tradition.

In his pioneering study on the history of the components of the Eucharist, the great liturgical scholar and promoter of the Liturgical Movement Joseph Andreas Jungmann describes *psalmi idiotici* as "for the most part, rude creations," which, "like the biblical psalms and canticles are not constructed on rhythmic and metrical principles." In terms of vocabulary, too, "they hold pretty close to their biblical models."[81] However, precisely in the combination of heterogeneous elements from Scripture, paraphrases, and allusions alongside word-for-word quotations, a new synthesis arises.

In the manuscript tradition, different versions of the *Gloria in excelsis Deo* are attested. Among other sources, the text is preserved in Greek in the *Apostolic Constitutions* and the Codex Alexandrinus,[82] which is important for our knowledge about the formation of the canon of biblical books and for editions of the Greek source text of the Bible. The mere fact that the Gloria appears in such a document shows how closely the text is related to the use of Scripture in worship.

Originally, the Gloria did not belong to the register of the Eucharist. It was a morning hymn in the register of the hours and came into being in the Christian East, as is evident from a homily by John Chrysostom.[83] Scholars agree that it was shifted from the hours to the Eucharist under the influence of conflicts over orthodoxy, in particular over the position of Christ vis-à-vis God the Father (cf. infra). The fourth-century Church father Hilary of Poitiers is supposed to have played a role in introducing the hymn to the West.

In terms of its use, it needs to be said that there has always been a peculiar sense of reverence for the Gloria. At first it was reserved for the solemnity of Christmas and it was the bishop only, not ordinary priests, who was allowed to sing it. Later on, in the early sixth century, its use was extended to Sundays and feasts of martyrs, but there are sources pointing to the fact that this was not the case during lent and advent. At a later stage, priests could sing the Gloria only in the first mass after their ordination. It is highly uncertain that the congregation was ever actively involved in the singing of the Gloria, which may not be ideal from a contemporary point of view but which does underscore the special status of the Gloria in the tradition.

---

[81] Joseph Andreas Jungmann, *The Mass of the Roman Rite: Its Origins and Development (Missarum Sollemnia)*, vol. 1 (Notre Dame: Ave Maria Press, 2012), 346–347.

[82] Bernard Cappelle, "Le texte du 'Gloria in excelsis'," *Revue d'histoire ecclésiastique* 44 (1949) 439–457. Meticulously showing different redactions of the text, Cappelle argued that the Codex Alexandrinus best keeps the original text of the Gloria.

[83] Taft, *The Liturgy of the Hours*, 82.

In the course of history the Gloria became part of the *ordinarium* of the Mass, together with the Kyrie, the Credo, the Sanctus, and the Agnus Dei. Occupying the second place in this series of five "songs" which remain identical in every solemn mass, it has been put on music by numerous composers. It would lead one too far to investigate this, but the creative ways in which composers have worked with the peculiar text material of the Gloria could reveal interesting insights, probably also in view of the topic of monotheism. What makes a lot of sense theologically is what the eighteenth-century Venetian priest at San Marco's Antonio Vivaldi did, in his famous Gloria, which is not part of a mass composition. In the last part, beginning with *Quoniam*, he repeats the theme of the first part, which obviously started with *Gloria*. This works admirably well qua sounds for the choir, but it supports the overall theological program of the hymn: only God, only Christ, is worthy of worship.

Below the Latin version of the Gloria is shown as it appears in the Missale Romanum of the Catholic Church.[84] The English translation is taken from the Roman Missal as well, notably from the third typical edition which appeared in the Anglophone world in the advent of 2011.[85] To make easy referencing possible, the text is presented here as containing five parts (Table 3). Usually, however, a twofold structure is adopted, a first part with a focus on the Father (A–C) and a second one focusing on Christ (D–E).

Table 3 The full text of the *Gloria in excelsis Deo*

Latin text	**English translation**
A/ *Gloria in excelsis Deo et in terra pax hominibus bonae voluntatis.*	Glory to God in the highest, and on earth peace to people of good will.
B/ *Laudamus te, benedicimus te, adoramus te, glorificamus te, gratias agimus tibi propter magnam gloriam tuam,*	We praise you, we bless you, we adore you, we glorify you, we give you thanks for your great glory,
C/ *Domine Deus, Rex caelestis, Deus Pater omnipotens.*	Lord God, heavenly King, O God, almighty Father.

---

[84] *Missale Romanum*, editio typica tertia, reimpressio emendata (Città del Vaticano: Libreria Editrice Vaticana, 2008), 509–510; OM, #8.

[85] *The Roman Missal*, 521–522; OM, #8.

Table 3 (cont.)

Latin text	English translation
D/ *Domine Fili Unigenite, Iesu Christe,*	Lord Jesus Christ, Only Begotten Son,
Domine Deus, Agnus Dei, Filius Patris,	Lord God, Lamb of God, Son of the Father,
qui tollis peccata mundi,	you take away the sins of the world,
miserere nobis,	have mercy on us;
qui tollis peccata mundi,	you take away the sins of the world,
suscipe deprecationem nostram.	receive our prayer;
Qui sedes ad dexteram Patris,	you are seated at the right hand of the Father,
miserere nobis.	have mercy on us.
E/ *Quoniam tu solus Sanctus,*	For you alone are the Holy One,
tu solus Dominus,	you alone are the Lord,
tu solus Altissimus,	you alone are the Most High,
Iesu Christe,	Jesus Christ,
cum Sancto Spiritu:	with the Holy Spirit,
in gloria Dei Patris.	in the glory of God the Father.
Amen.	Amen.

The opening lines of the Gloria are a literal quotation from the second chapter of the gospel of Luke (v. 14). The context in which this text appears is the story of Christmas. It is the angels of heaven whose song of praise is suddenly heard when the shepherds receive the message from one angel that they will find the Savior in their immediate surroundings, however not in a majestic manner but as a newborn child in a manger. For this very reason the Gloria is also called the angelic hymn.

Within the gospel of Luke there is an interesting parallel to these words, where there is also an elevated acclamation and the emphatic combination of peace and glory.[86] The context now is Palm Sunday, where not the angels but the multitude of Jesus' disciples starts to praise God loudly when they approach Jerusalem. They use the following words: "Blessed is the king who comes in the name of the Lord! Peace in heaven, and glory in the highest heaven" (Lk 19:38). This textual connection is not a coincidence. Shortly after the beginning of Christ's life and shortly before it ends, God is praised for his mighty intervention for people. The enigma of this mightiness is that it is manifested in the vulnerable life of a human person. There is an implicit understanding that there

---

[86] Cf. Agape Kiesgen, "Die große Doxologie der Kirche," *Bibel und Liturgie* 2 (1927/1928) 273–279, 320–326, 274–275.

is only one such person, Jesus, in whom God has revealed ultimately His love, that is, His firm intention to save humankind.

The concept of glory, *doxa*, appears three times in the text of the Gloria. It does so at significant moments, at the beginning, at the end, and somewhere in the middle. The literary function of this pattern could be a double inclusion. Glory wraps up the whole text, parts A–E (cf. Table 3). But glory also wraps up parts A and B, where one has five successive verbs in the first person plural, all expressing the human willingness to worship God. The activities expressed through these verbs correspond with what is being asked in section D of the hymn, that God extends His mercy and accepts human petitions. Soteriology and doxology work here as two sides of the same coin; God's saving mercy (on earth) corresponds with His glory (in heaven). And humans express their desire to share in both.

With respect to the issue of monotheism two elements from the text of the Gloria stand out. First, there is the explicit address of both the almighty Father, king of heaven, and the only begotten Son, the Lamb of God, as *Domine Deus*, "Lord God" (in C and in the opening words of D). From a logical point of view, the question can be raised who then the Lord God is, Father or Son, assuming that it must be one subject only of whom divine lordship is predicated. Again, however, as was the case with the Christological interpretation of the psalms, the confession of Jesus Christ's lordship as not in any way different from God's lordship in the context of elevated doxologies appears to be the crucial key to understand the specifically Christian kind of monotheism.

This is enhanced – and that is at once the second point – by the triple direct address "*tu (solus)*" with which Jesus Christ is acclaimed (E). The first address, "you alone are the Holy One," is – as was mentioned before – a literal quotation from Revelation 15:4, with holiness being a quality uniquely attributed to God. No one else or nothing else beside Him can claim this quality, and if it has this quality it is by virtue of participation in the divine holiness. The second address once more highlights Jesus Christ's lordship, which he fundamentally and consistently shares with the Father.

The emphasis on Christ being *Dominus*, *kurios* in Greek, is to a large extent dependent on the Pauline corpus. This idea is further accentuated by saying that only Christ is *Altissimus*, the Most High, that is, God Himself. Nothing else is higher, and this highest highness is shared with nobody else. As is made clear in the Letter to the Colossians: "For in him [i.e., Christ Jesus the Lord] the whole fullness of deity dwells bodily, and you have come to fullness in him, who is the head of every ruler and authority" (Col 2:9–10). This latter phrase puts forward the idea that no worldly power whatsoever, not even – and especially not – the ones who claim divine descent or status, can be worshiped by Christians. God only is praised.

At present the Gloria is used in the Roman rite in every celebration of the Eucharist on Sundays and feast days, with the exception of lent and advent.[87] The custom not to have the Gloria during the times of preparation for Easter and Christmas goes centuries back but also has a deep theological and spiritual meaning. Of course, at Christmas, it profiles the fact that the first words of the hymn are taken from the Christmas narrative in the gospel of Luke. It also preserves some of the age-old reverence for the solemn words that are used, especially the honorary titles for God and Christ. In addition, however, in the specific context of the Eucharist, the regulation to reserve the Gloria for the most important occasions in the liturgical life of the Church reinforces the exceptional character of God's glory, which is not ordinary at all. To express God's glory with so special words requires specific contexts; it cannot be done just at any time by any individual. Furthermore, this regulation highlights that singing the unique praises that are due to God only is particularly appropriate on the occasion of remembering the incarnation and resurrection of His Son.

With respect to the second *psalmus idioticus* under consideration, the *Te Deum laudamus*, similar points as the ones made about the *Gloria in excelsis Deo* will be developed. Although the text of the hymn is longer (Table 4), however, the commentary can be shorter. The English translation of the text is taken from the breviary put together by Maxwell Johnson;[88] the Latin original can be found in any pre-Vatican II breviary.

Like the Gloria, the Te Deum is not meant for every celebration but reserved for special occasions. Other than Gloria, however, it has never become an element of the Eucharistic celebration. It has always stayed in the regime of the liturgy of the hours, where it is sung on Sundays outside lent and on feasts in the hours of matins, now usually called the office of readings. Because of its length, the rubrics say that the last part of the hymn, "that is, from the verse, *Save your people, Lord* to the end, may be omitted."[89]

---

[87] Christian Müller, Jörg Müller, Annette Traber, and Ralph Walterspacher, "Gloria," in *Gemeinsam vor Gott treten: Die Liturgie mit biblischen Augen betrachten*, Luzerner Biblisch-Liturgischer Kommentar zum Ordo Missae, vol. 1, ed. Birgit Jeggle-Merz, Walter Kirchschläger, and Jörg Müller (Stuttgart: Katholisches Bibelwerk, 2014), 109–143.

[88] *Benedictine Daily Prayer*, 906–908.

[89] *General Instruction of the Liturgy of the Hours*, #68; *The Liturgy Documents*, vol. 2, 282.

Table 4 The full text of the *Te Deum laudaus*

Latin text	English translation
A/ *Te Deum laudamus* *te Dominum confitemur* *Te aeternum Patrem* *omnis terra veneratur.* *Tibi omnes Angeli* *tibi caeli et universae potestates* *tibi Cherubim et Seraphim incessabili voce* *proclamant*	We appraise you, O God; we acclaim you Lord and Master. Everlasting Father, all the world bows down before you. All the angels sing your praise, the hosts of heaven and all the angelic powers; All the cherubim and seraphim call out to you in unending chorus:
B/ *Sanctus, sanctus, sanctus Dominus, Deus Sabaoth.* *Pleni sunt celi et terra maiestatis gloriae tuae.*	Holy, holy, holy is the Lord God of angel hosts! The heavens and the earth are filled, Lord, with your majesty and glory.
C/ *Te gloriosus Apostolorum chorus* *Te Prophetarum laudabilis numerus* *Te Martyrum candidatus laudat exercitus.*	Your praises are sung by the renowned Apostles; By all the prophets, who themselves deserve our praise; By that mighty white-robed army who shed their blood for Christ.

D/ *Te per orbem terrarum*
sancta confitetur Ecclesia,
Patrem
immense maiestatis;
venerandum tuum
verum unicum Filium;
Sanctum quoque Paraclitum Spiritum.

E/ *Tu Rex gloriae, Christe.*
Tu Patris sempiternus es Filius.
Tu, ad liberandum suscepturus hominem,
Non horruisti Virginis uterum.
Tu, devicto mortis aculeo,
aperuisti credentibus regna caelorum
Tu ad dexteram Dei sedes,
in gloria Patris.

F/ *Iudex crederis esse venturus.*
Te ergo quaesumus, tuis famulis subveni,
quos pretioso sanguine redemisti.
Aeterna fac cum Sanctis tuis in gloria munerari.

D/ And to the ends of the earth,
the holy Church proclaims her faith in you:
Father,
whose majesty is boundless;
Your only Son,
who is true God who is to be adored;
The Holy Spirit,
sent to be our Advocate.

E/ O Christ, the King of glory!
You alone are the Father's eternal Son.
When you became man so as to save humankind,
you did not shrink back from the chaste virgin's womb.
When you triumphantly destroyed death's sting,
you opened up to believers the kingdom of heaven.
You are now enthroned at God's right hand, in
the Father's glory.

F/ We believe that you will come for judgment.
We therefore implore you to grant your servants grace and aid,
for you shed your precious blood for their redemption.
Admit them all to the ranks of your saints in everlasting glory.

Table 4 (cont.)

Latin text	English translation
Salvum fac populum tuum, Domine, et benedic hereditati tuae.	Be the Savior of your faithful people, Lord; grant them your blessing, for they belong to you.
Et rege eos et extolle illos usque in aeternum.	Be their Shepherd, Lord, uphold and exalt them forever and ever.
G/ Per singulos dies benedicimus te; et laudamus nomen tuum in saeculum et in saeculum saeculi.	Day by day we praise you, daily we acclaim you. We will confess and glorify your holy name, now and for all eternity.
Dignare, Domine, die isto, sine peccato nos custodire.	In your great mercy, Lord, throughout this day keep us from sin by your protection.
Miserere nostri, Domine, miserere nostri.	Have mercy on us, we humbly pray; Lord, have mercy on us.
Fiat misericordia tua, Domine, super nos quemadmodum speravimus in te	May your mercy, Lord, your loving-kindness, always remain with us; for we have placed our confidence in you.
In te, Domine, speravi: non confundar in aeternum.	In you alone, Lord I have hoped; may I not be disappointed.

The Te Deum opens with a direct address of God, who is praised and confessed as Lord and Father. What follows (A–D, cf. Table 4) is an enumeration of who is involved in this action of rendering honor to God. The enumeration follows a classical pattern of the celestial hierarchy of angels and saints. The text mentions particular categories such as the cherubim and seraphim, the apostles, the prophets and the martyrs. All of them are involved in the heavenly praise, which the church on earth joins in.

Inasmuch as one section of the Te Deum is the Sanctus (B), there is an obvious connection here with the Eucharist. The preface of the Eucharistic prayer culminates in the Sanctus, emphasizing the connection the liturgical assembly makes with the heavenly Church and in particular with the angels. Liturgically speaking, the angels are the real professionals of praise: all they do, all the time, without interruption or being distracted, is singing for God's glory. From their activity the entire heaven and full earth are filled with that glory. What the Church does when she gathers for worship and sings the Te Deum is, symbolically, sharing in that eternal activity of glorification.

The first part of the text (A–D) ends with a Trinitarian doxology, like almost every Christian liturgical prayer. Like the Gloria's first part, it revolves around the worship of God the Father. And like the Gloria's second part, the Te Deum's second part shifts the attention to Jesus Christ and his redemptive work. Again, doxology smoothly flows over into soteriology, and is actually extended and exemplified by it. Christ's *oikonomia* cannot be eliminated from God's *theologia*, and therefore the Son's glory absolutely equals the Father's. This is particularly expressed by the inclusion of the word glory in part E: Christ is the king of glory and is seated at God's right hand, in glory.

Even if the fundamental message of the Te Deum in terms of the praise that is due to God only, Father and Son, is not different from the Gloria, these two *psalmi idiotici* have had another reception history. In his inaugural address as professor at the University of Bonn, the renowned German liturgist Albert Gerhards recalled that, already at the time of the Carolingians, the Te Deum was used for public expressions of gratitude and, interwoven with them, many different festivities and ceremonies. It was a hymn in which the clergy had a privileged role – the laity responded with simple Kyries – but it received its extraordinary status above all as it became a part of royal ordinations and enthronement rituals.[90] As a consequence, the Te Deum was blurred with state ideologies and their nationalisms. In spite of its superb musical quality, this is precisely what is shown in the famous Te Deum by seventeenth-century

---

[90] Albert Gerhards, "Te Deum laudamus – Die Marseillaise der Kirche? Ein christlicher Hymnus im Spannungsfeld von Liturgie und Politik," *Liturgisches Jarhbuch* 40 (1990) 65–77, 71.

French composer Marc-Antoine Charpentier. Actually, Charpentier composed four Te Deums, but he is most known for the instrumental overture that many people recognize as the tune of the Eurovision song contest. The music itself plainly resonates with the military victories of a powerful regime.

Despite this loaded history, Gerhards appreciates the fact that the text of the Te Deum is solidly engrafted on biblical language, whence it can be used as a model for contemporary Christian praying and singing. He goes on to say that, because of this background, the Te Deum in particular and the Christian liturgy more generally can contribute to questioning mechanisms of power which one so often sees occurring in national and international politics. He contends: "Against all holistic utopias of salvation and systems of self-redemption, the Church has to proclaim the hope of incorruptibility – and that on the initiative of God: *in te domine speravi non confundar in aeternum*,"[91] thereby referring to the last lines of the Te Deum.

With respect to monotheism, this application of the meaning of a classical liturgical text to today makes a lot of sense. It ties in with De Kesel's insight that monotheism implies a rupture in the rule of anything. Therefore, the deep doxological nature of both the Gloria and the Te Deum is highly relevant. As is the fact that they reserve praise to the one Dominus only, who is God *and* Christ. It may be hard to grasp from a purely logical point of view, but from a *doxo*-logical point of view, the confession, proclamation, and acclamation of the oneness of the Lord as both Father and Son constitutes the beating heart of Christian liturgy. James Chrichton's insight, which he only applied to the psalms, can therefore now be unhesitatingly verified on the basis of a reading of the two most influential *psalmi idiotici* of the Christian liturgical tradition: the genius of Christian prayer consists in identifying the praise to the Son and the praise to the Father, and to thereby confirm biblical monotheism.

3.3 The Doxologies Concluding the Eucharistic Prayers or Anaphoras

The next field of inquiry is the Eucharistic prayer. Whereas the first paragraph of this section dealt with the liturgy of the hours, especially with psalms and hymns, and the second one with hymns at the crossroads of the hours and the Eucharist, the present section consistently focuses on the Eucharist. And within the regime of the Eucharist, it centers on the Eucharistic prayer, also called the anaphora. Literally, the word "anaphora," derived from the Greek verb *ana-pherein*, refers to the action of carrying something upward, as does the Latin word "oblation" (from the verb *offerre*). It could be argued theologically that

---

[91] Gerhards, "Te Deum laudamus," 77 (my translation, JG).

what is brought up is human praise for God. In any case, the Eucharist as a whole is profoundly doxological.

The Eucharistic prayer constitutes a core element of the celebration of the Eucharist since the very beginnings of the Christian religion. It is mentioned by second-century apologist Justin the Martyr and is supposed to have roots in second-temple Jewish meal practices, where the food and the wine were blessed. In the period between the writing of the books of the New Testament and the fourth century CE, when Christians were no longer threatened by the outbreak of persecutions in the Roman Empire, and when it enjoyed a particular time of flourishing, so-called paleo-anaphora were developed. This concept refers to the stage between the earliest forms of Christian liturgical life and the emergence of full anaphoras of which we have textual witnesses.[92]

It seems that doxologies have been put at the beginning and the end of each anaphora. In the Eucharistic prayers that influenced Western Christianity, many of which had links with the East, the first part of them culminated in the Sanctus. The meaning of that practice is explained, among others, in the mystagogical catecheses of Cyril of Jerusalem, who was the bishop there in the later part of the fourth century CE: "We say this doxology, which was given to us by the seraphim, in order that by sharing this hymn we may be associated with the heavenly hosts."[93] On the basis of this parallel, Gerhards rightly remarked a striking parallel between the Te Deum and the Eucharistic Prayer.[94]

Below, however, attention will be paid to the concluding formulae of Eucharistic prayers, because they more specifically lay bare a monotheistic pattern. Other than the dominant logic we found in the *psalmi idiotici*, assuring the equal divinity of Son and Father, but certainly not contradictory to them, is the more fully developed, though surprisingly concise, Trinitarian logic in the final doxologies of the anaphoral tradition. There is a remarkable consistency with respect to the ways in which the oneness of God as Father, Son, and Holy Spirit is expressed. The sources referred to below are all taken from the standard edition of anaphoras in English by Ronald Jasper and Geoffrey Cuming.[95]

---

[92] The literature about this constitutive phase in the development of the Eucharist is abundant. Suffice it here to mention the following works: Eugene LaVerdiere, *The Eucharist in the New Testament and the Early Church* (Collegeville: Liturgical Press, 1996); Enrico Mazza, *The Celebration of the Eucharist: The Origins of the Rite and the Development of Its Interpretation*, trans. Matthew J. O'Connell (Collegeville: Liturgical Press, 1999); Paul F. Bradshaw and Maxwell E. Johnson, *The Eucharistic Liturgies: Their Evolution and Interpretation* (Collegeville: Liturgical Press, 2012).

[93] Quoted in Mazza, *The Celebration of the Eucharist*, 287.

[94] Gerhards, "Te Deum laudamus," 67.

[95] Ronald C. D. Jasper and Geoffrey J. Cuming, *Prayers of the Eucharist: Early and Reformed*, 3rd ed. (Collegeville: Liturgical Press, 1990).

In the Byzantine liturgical tradition, two Eucharistic prayers are used. The one is named after Cappadocian Basil the Great, the other one after John Chrysostom. Both texts have a venerable history, but what is interesting to note is that they have exactly the same doxological ending:

> [G]rant us with one mouth and one heart to glorify and hymn your all-honorable and magnificent name, the Father and the Son and the Holy Spirit, now <and always and to the ages of ages>. *People*: Amen.[96]

In the Roman rite, it was the Roman canon which for centuries determined the identity of the mass, since it was the only Eucharistic prayer in this tradition. How and when exactly it came into being is not known with precision, but it is not unlikely that this happened during the fourth century in Rome. This was a time when many liturgical services were codified by means of formularies and forms, and when there was a shift from the Greek to the Latin language in the liturgy.[97] The text of the Roman canon concludes as follows:

> Through him, Lord, you ever create, sanctify, quicken, bless, and bestow all these good things upon us. Through him and with him and in him all honor and glory is yours, O God the Father almighty, in the unity of the Holy Spirit, through all the ages of ages. Amen.[98]

It is believed that the earliest textual traces of the Roman canon are found in the mystagogical catecheses of Ambrose of Milan as written down in his *De sacramentis* (*On the Sacraments*). The similarity with the above quoted final doxology of the Roman canon is indeed striking:

> Through our Lord Jesus Christ, in whom and with whom honor, praise, glory, magnificence, and power are yours, with the Holy Spirit, from the ages, and now, and always, and to all the ages of ages. Amen.[99]

Also striking is how close these formulations, taken from ancient sources, are with the present doxologies of the Eucharistic prayers in the Roman missal. Since the liturgical reforms of Vatican II, there is more than one anaphora. Depending on how one counts and which status one grants to the appendix to the Ordo Missae, there are at present no less than ten Eucharistic prayers. All of them have exactly the same doxological ending, however, which is clearly taken from the Roman canon. For Catholics going regularly to mass its sounds very familiar:

---

[96] Jasper and Cuming, *Prayers of the Eucharist*, 123, 134.

[97] Enrizo Mazza, *The Eucharistic Prayers of the Roman Rite*, trans. Matthew J. O'Connell (Collegeville: Liturgical Press, 2004), 53–59.

[98] Jasper and Cuming, *Prayers of the Eucharist*, 166.

[99] Jasper and Cuming, *Prayers of the Eucharist*, 146.

Through him, and with him, and in him,
O God, almighty Father,
in the unity of the Holy Spirit,
all glory and honor is yours,
for ever and ever. Amen.[100]

In the Latin original of the Missale Romanum, which for this component does not in any way differ from the missal from before the liturgical reforms, this is:

Per ipsum, et cum ipso, et in ipso,
est tibi Deo Patri omnipotenti,
in unitate Spiritus Sancti,
omnis honor et gloria
per omnia saecula saeculorum. Amen.[101]

The very pattern to end the anaphora with a Trinitarian doxology was perpetuated in the Reformation, even if the content of the Eucharistic prayers was sometimes drastically changed because of doctrinal considerations. In the 1549 Book of Common Prayer as well as in the 1552 version of it, despite many smaller and bigger differences between both, the same doxological formula concludes the Eucharistic prayer:

through Christ our Lord; by whom, and with whom, in the unity of the Holy Ghost, all honour and glory be unto thee, O Father almighty, world without end. Amen.[102]

This wording continues to be modeled after the Roman canon, which is not the case in the more radical Reformation. What does not change, however, is the fact that one keeps the anaphora as a constitutive part of the celebration of the Lord's Supper and that one has it end with a Trinitarian doxology. By way of illustration, a reference can be made to John Knox's The Form of Prayers, which was introduced in Scotland in the 1560s and in which the influence of John Calvin is apparent.

And these most inestimable gifts, we acknowledge and confess to have received of thy free mercy and grace, by thy only beloved Son Jesus Christ,

---

[100] *The Roman Missal,* 643, 649, 654, 662; OM, #98, #106, #114, #123. These are the references to the doxologies of the four Eucharistic prayers which are part of the Ordo Missae since 1969. The ones which were later adopted and put in the appendix do have the same doxology without exception.

[101] *Missale Romanum,* 579; OM, #98. For an interesting though already somewhat older study, see Camille Callewaert, "La finale du canon de la messe," *Revue d'histoire ecclésiastique* 39 (1943) 5–21. Callewaert notifies that the formulation contains *est* in the indicative form, thus not a subjunctive verb form such as *sit,* and emphasizes the importance of the prepositions *per, cum,* and *in.* According to him, this threefold pattern underscores the Christological mediation of the entire Eucharistic action as well as the substantial unity of the Son and the Father, as is elsewhere made explicit in the mass, in particular in the creed.

[102] Jasper and Cuming, *Prayers of the Eucharist,* 240, 249. Cf. also the version from the 1637 Scottish Book of Common Prayer: Jaspers and Cuming, *Prayers of the Eucharist,* 263.

for the which therefore we thy congregation moved by the Holy Spirit render thee all thanks, praise, and glory for ever and ever.[103]

What all of these doxologies at the end of the Eucharistic prayer have in common is a concern about the oneness of God and the unity of the three divine persons. Therefore, these doxologies are exemplary and essential to comprehend how the liturgy expresses Christian monotheism. Two thoughts may summarize the thrust of the anaphoral doxologies.

First, there is no doubt that the ultimate addressee of the Eucharistic prayer is God the Father. Yet almost everything which is said further on in the prayer circles around Jesus Christ, the Son of the Father. The *oikonomia* of Christ's redemption is colorfully remembered and the Holy Spirit is called upon to sanctify the gifts of bread and wine brought to the altar. This *anamnetic* and *epicletic* context is essential for the institution narrative including the words of consecration to be recited.[104] All of this material, however, needs to be brought to a proper conclusion or synthesis. And that is exactly what the final doxology does, by insisting that Christ's work of salvation and the human participation in that made possible by the Holy Spirit are not in any way deviating from God the Father's reaching out to humankind.

Second, the doxology at the end to the anaphora makes it clear that Christian liturgical prayer is a complex and dynamic activity. It is quite a challenge to imagine how Christ's life, words, death, and resurrection are connected to God's life and love, and to maintain a strict monotheism. Therefore, there cannot be too much variation in the doxological phrases. In one way or another, they express the fundamental idea that, actually, human praise of God is inserted in the Son's praise of the Father, and that it is the Holy Spirit who guarantees the unity and divine focus of all this praise. What Mazza says with reference to the Roman canon may therefore be extrapolated to other doxologies at the end of Eucharistic prayers:

> Everything belongs to the Father. All honor and glory ascends to him in a Christocentric movement that is expressed by three prepositions: "Through, with, in." Our celebration, like our very life, derives all its value and meaning from its Christ-centeredness. The doxology makes this thought its own and broadens it to include all things. This honor and glory ascend to him "in the unity of the Holy Spirit," not only because the only acceptable worship is that in Spirit and in truth, but also and above all because the unity of God enters into us through that same Spirit.[105]

It is interesting to note that in concrete celebrations of the liturgy the posture of both presider and congregation at the doxologies is normally standing upright.

---

[103] Jasper and Cuming, *Prayers of the Eucharist*, 256.

[104] Cesare Giraudo, *In unum corpus: Traité mystagogique sur l'Eucharistie*, trans. Éric Iborra and Pierre-Marie Hombert (Paris: Cerf, 2014).

[105] Mazza, *The Eucharistic Prayers of the Roman Rite*, 87.

The symbolic meaning of this bodily posture is a reference to the resurrection. As a participant in the celebration one takes on the position of standing-up, of *ana-stasis*, when God's praises for His mighty deeds are expressed. This is moreover not only the case for the doxologies at the end of the Eucharistic prayer, but also for the Gloria, as part of the introductory rites of the mass, and the Te Deum in the liturgy of the hours, where this hymn takes on a place similar to the evangelic canticles in lauds, vespers, and compline.

Furthermore, the meaning of this bodily posture is augmented by the "Amen," which is the typical one-word response to the doxologies concluding the anaphoras. Mazza explains: "The 'Amen' of the faithful is very important, because it ratifies the anaphora uttered by the priest. The final 'Amen' is as it were a seal on the celebration of the Eucharist, which is by definition the sacrament of the unity of the Church."[106] The Eucharist, however, is equally the sacrament par excellence where the uniqueness of God is celebrated. Therefore, this same "Amen" by the whole gathered assembly can additionally be considered a liturgical seal on Christian monotheism.

4 The Unity of Father, Son, and Holy Spirit in the Orations

The above explorations of the *Gloria Patri* or little doxology – as it is often called – at the end the praying of the psalms, the greater doxology or *Gloria in excelsis*, and the doxological formula concluding the anaphora in the Eucharist, have delivered a dynamic picture of the ways in which Christians' profound monotheistic conviction is embodied and expressed in the liturgy. The crucial factor in this monotheism was the confession that the worship of Jesus Christ as the Lord is the same as the worship of God the Father. One could even go one step further and claim that, in Christian liturgy, the worship of the Father is lacking crucial content if nothing is said with reference to the Son (and the Holy Spirit).

From a historical point of view, however, the confluence of the worship of the Father with the worship of the Son has been an extraordinarily complicated matter. The "correct" way of praying – orthodox liturgy – has been the subject of acrimonious debates. In a way, what Lohfink says is quite soothing: "We don't have to remember constantly that we are praying *through* Jesus Christ *in* the Holy Spirit. [...] Likewise the liturgy, with its doxologies, constantly reminds us of this basic structure of all prayer."[107] However, this consolation does not relieve us from the duty to take a closer look at the orations and to see whether a similar pattern of ascribing what is said about the Son to the Father can be discovered there, too.

---

[106] Mazza, *The Celebration of the Eucharist*, 295. Cf. also Giraudo, *In unum corpus*, 396–400.
[107] Lohfink, *Prayer Takes Us Home*, 25.

The orations are a particular group of liturgical prayers in the Roman rite. They occur both in the Eucharist and in the liturgy of the hours and are in principle said aloud by the person presiding at the assembly, usually the priest. For that reason the orations are also called presidential prayers. In the regime of the Eucharist, there are three orations, each bringing to a conclusion a series of rites: (1) the collect(a) or opening prayer, which concludes the introductory rites, (2) the prayer over the offerings, which concludes the preparation of the gifts and the altar (previously called the offertory [rites]), and (3) the prayer after communion, which concludes the communion rites.

Together with some other liturgical material, the orations give shape to mass forms. For every celebration of the Eucharist in the Roman rite, there is a mass form, depending on the kind of mass one celebrates (Sunday mass, weekday mass, feast or solemnity, ritual mass, votive mass, etc.). The historical and philological study as well as the theological interpretation of these orations is an important task of the liturgical subfield named euchology.

Euchological studies of the liturgical material present in the Roman missal have revealed the surprisingly heterogeneous origins of the prayer texts used. It is only a minority of them which can with certainty be said to have their origin in the city of Rome and its immediate surroundings. What is more important for our topic of monotheism, however, than the diverse contents and various origins of the orations, is the fact that many of them were originally addressed to the Father, that others were originally addressed to the Son, and – above all – that intriguing interventions were made to splice these two directions together in order to preserve both traditional biblical monotheism and Trinitarian faith.

What this means concretely can best be shown by sketching a contrast between two examples. For all the texts of the orations the following reference is made to the Roman missal. The three orations for the solemnity of the Most Holy Trinity, which is celebrated in the Catholic Church on the first Sunday after Pentecost, are addressed to the Father. The collect for this feast is the following:

> God our Father, who by sending into the world the Word of truth and the Spirit of sanctification made known to the human race your wondrous mystery, grant us, we pray, that in professing the true faith, we may acknowledge the Trinity of eternal glory and adore your Unity, powerful in majesty. Through our Lord Jesus Christ, your Son, who lives and reigns with you in the unity of the Holy Spirit, one God, for ever and ever.[108]

This prayer is particularly well crafted, and an important reference for the overall argument about monotheism developed in this Element. The prayer is addressed *to* the Father, *through* the Son, *in* the unity of the Holy Spirit. In that

---

[108] *The Roman Missal*, 495.

sense it is illustrative of liturgical prayer as a whole (cf. infra). Furthermore, in the opening two lines of the prayer an explicit reference is made to the three persons constituting the Trinity (the Father, the Word – i.e., the Son – and the Spirit), which, however, constitute one mystery. This mystery is received in faith and is doxological from a to z, inasmuch as it consists in rendering glory to God, who is at the same time, and always, three and one. This oneness is strengthened by the standard closing formula, not only by referring to the Holy Spirit maintaining the unity, but also by the fact that "one God, for ever and ever" is added. It seems that this monotheist confession is essential for the liturgy to remain within the boundaries of adequate doxology, or indeed orthodoxy.

In the prayer over the offerings on the feast of the Holy Trinity, the "Lord" in question is clearly God the Father. The prayer is not completed, however, without the addition that what is prayed is done through the "Lord," in this case the Son.

> Sanctify by the invocation of your name,
> we pray, O Lord our God,
> this oblation of our service,
> and by it make of us an eternal offering to you.
> Through Christ our Lord.[109]

One observes the same pattern in the prayer after communion: intriguingly, both the Father and the Son are explicitly called "our Lord." In addition, this particular prayer provides yet another beautiful example of Christian monotheism as expressed through the liturgy, in the sense that there is a full equivocation of God's "holy Trinity" and "undivided Unity."

> May receiving this Sacrament, O Lord our God,
> bring us health of body and soul,
> as we confess your eternal holy Trinity and undivided Unity.
> Through Christ our Lord.[110]

In the orations of the solemnity of the Body and Blood of Christ, probably better known as the feast of Corpus Christi, one sees a different pattern. Not every oration is addressed to the Father, with the addition that the community actually prays "through" the mediation of the Son. The collect of Corpus Christi is an excellent example of an oration directed to Christ:

> O God, who in this wonderful Sacrament
> have left us a memorial of your Passion,
> grant us, we pray,
> so to revere the sacred mysteries of your Body and Blood
> that we may always experience in ourselves

---

[109] *The Roman Missal*, 495.   [110] *The Roman Missal*, 498.

>the fruits of your redemption.
>Who live and reign with God the Father
>in the unity of the Holy Spirit,
>one God, for ever and ever.[111]

When an oration is addressed to Son instead of the Father, the concluding formula changes. In such cases their "living and reigning" together, typically divine activities, are highlighted. What is implied by this formula is that there is no difference between the Son's and the Father's being and life, and that also their ruling is essentially the same. This sameness is unambiguously enhanced by the appeal to the unity of the Holy Spirit, and again there is the addition of "one God," which may not be necessary from a purely logical point of view. But from a doxological and a euchological point of view, an extra clarification is only beneficial.

The prayer over the offerings on the feast of Corpus Christi is a typical one, addressed to the Father "through" the Son, both being equally and unequivocally "Lord."

>Grant your Church, O Lord, we pray,
>the gifts of unity and peace,
>whose signs are to be seen in mystery
>in the offerings we here present.
>Through Christ our Lord.[112]

The prayer after communion is again directed to the Son, which is made evident, as was the case also in the collect, through the reference to the body and blood. Because it is addressed to Christ already, the prayer does not need the concluding formula "through our Lord Jesus Christ (etc.)."

>Grant, O Lord, we pray,
>that we may delight for all eternity
>in that share in your divine life,
>which is foreshadowed in the present age
>by our reception of your precious Body and Blood.
>Who live and reign for ever and ever.[113]

In the current version of the Roman missal, these euchological specifications have somehow become evident. The formulae to end the orations with, whether they are addressed to God the Father or to God the Son, have become solid and transparent, and thus recognizable. In a concise, precise, and consistent manner, they reflect the doxological basic structure of Christian liturgy, a firm faith in the Trinity, and a clear monotheistic image of God.[114] This situation, however, has

---

[111] *The Roman Missal*, 499.   [112] *The Roman Missal*, 499.   [113] *The Roman Missal*, 501.

[114] In this context it is relevant to additionally refer to the *General Instruction of the Roman Missal*, #54; *The Roman Missal*, 31. It is explained which the standard ending formulae are of the

not always been the case. There was a lot of debate over these formulae in early Christianity, especially from the late third and in the fourth centuries CE, that is, at a time when there were harsh controversies surrounding the major Christological and Trinitarian doctrines. There were, at the same time, equally discussions among scholars about these early Christian debates. It is important to briefly refer to these discussions, since they can teach us something important about the peculiar way in which monotheism is expressed in Christian liturgies.

In a much too schematic way, someone like Camille Callewaert supposed that the doxological formula typical of the West was *Gloria Patri et Filio et Spiritui Sancto*, with a straightforward juxtaposition of the three divine persons, and that in the East this was rather *Gloria Patri per Filium in Spiritu Sancto*,[115] expressing a dynamic movement. However, it was Jungmann who first came up with a comprehensive theory. In a thorough and groundbreaking study, which originally dates from 1925 already, he discussed the role and position of Christ in liturgical prayer.[116]

In the first part of his work, Jungmann gathered and discussed liturgical source material from the first centuries, both from the earliest texts such as the *Didachè* and from later developments in Syria, Egypt, and the West, particularly Rome. In the second part Jungmann unfolded some historical and theological claims about what he considered the dominant (and therefore orthodox) pattern of all the prayer expressions covered. Jungmann very strongly held that all liturgical prayer was directed *to* the Father (*ad Patrem*), *through* Christ (*per Christum*), and *in* the Spirit (*in Spiritum*), and that this was the case both in the East and in the West.

In prayers directly addressed to Christ (*ad Christum*) Jungmann saw deviant evolutions influenced either by heresies, primarily those of the Monophysites in the Syrian realm, or by overreactions against them, especially Arianism. Jungmann supposed that, whereas Arians denied the divinity of the Son, their Catholic or "orthodox" opponents overcorrected this by directing their public worship directly to Christ. Fundamental, however, for Jungmann was the unique and exclusive mediatorship of the Son, as expressed in Paul's first Letter to Timothy,[117] and the fact that the Roman church had stayed loyal to this basic conviction laid out in Scripture in the midst and in spite of so many

---

collecta prayer, depending on the question whether they are addressed to the Father or to the Son. (No oration is addressed to the Holy Spirit.)

[115] Callewaert, "La finale du canon," 18.

[116] Josef A. Jungmann, *The Place of Christ in Liturgical Prayer* (London: Geoffrey Chapman, 1989). The German title of this work is *Die Stellung Christi im liturgischen Gebet*.

[117] 1 Tim 2:3-6: "This is right and is acceptable in the sight of God our Savior, who desires everyone to be saved and to come to the knowledge of the truth. For there is one God; there is also one mediator between God and humankind, Christ Jesus, himself human, who gave himself a ransom for all – this was attested at the right time."

vicissitudes and painful conflicts. Jungmann additionally relied on explicit theological theories about authentic Christian prayer in the work of Origen.

Jungmann's theory is now outdated and has been severely criticized from several angles. It is no longer held that there was one solid pattern of prayer in Christians' worship services, which spread everywhere, and was kept in a special way in Rome. In addition, liturgical scholars, historians of the Church, and theologians today show great restraint when they speak of heresies and heterodoxy. They refrain from simplistic schemas and grand claims and prefer the evidence speak for itself. Accordingly, Bryan Spinks painstakingly pointed at the very selective use Jungmann made of both biblical and ancient liturgical sources, thus questioning some of his most basic assumptions. At the same time, Spinks perceptively reminded that Balthasar Fischer, who wrote a preface for the English reedition of Jungmann's work in 1989, said that "sound liturgical piety depends on both the *ad Christum* and the *per Christum*."[118]

Paul Bradshaw basically concurs with Spinks' criticism of Jungmann and observes that in early Christianity "it is clear that the alleged standard formula 'through Christ and in the Holy Spirit' was anything but universal."[119] He emphasizes that there were many emerging liturgical families at the time and that there was quite some variety among them in dealing with the central fact that underlying the New Testament is the conviction "that Jesus was the sole mediator through whom God's salvation had been brought to humankind" and that, as a consequence, it is hardly surprising "to find that he was also regarded there as the mediator through whom worship and praise were now to be offered to God."[120] In an intriguing and revealing way, the double pattern of doxology/ *theologia* and soteriology/*oikonomia* as fundamental for Christian worship here surfaces again.

Yet, the question remains how monotheism fits into these discussions. The renowned exegete and specialist of the primitive Church Larry Hurtado proposes for that reason to carefully look into the piety and devotion of the earliest Christians, which he thought was permeated by a salient reverence for the figure of Jesus Christ. This piety was not only smoothly adopted by the people but also actively stimulated by the leaders of their communities. Hurtado argues that "the early Christian understanding of God and of Jesus' relationship to God (the 'Father')

---

[118] Jungmann, *The Place of Christ*, x. Quoted in Bryan D. Spinks, "The Place of Christ in Liturgical Prayer: What Jungmann Omitted to Say," in *The Place of Christ in Liturgical Prayer: Trinity, Christology, and Liturgical Theology*, ed. Bryan D. Spinks (Collegeville: Liturgical Press, 2008), 1, 19.

[119] Paul Bradshaw, "God, Christ and the Holy Spirit in Early Christian Praying," in Spinks, *The Place of Christ*, 62.

[120] Bradshaw, "God, Christ and the Holy Spirit," 51.

were driven and shaped by the pattern of earliest Christian devotional practice."[121] He interestingly calls this pattern "binitarian," which is certainly not a denial of the Trinitarian faith of Christians, but rather a crucial development in it.

Hurtado uses the concept binitarian "to underscore the inclusion of Jesus with God as recipient of devotion," something which "early Christians characteristically refused to offer to other figures, whether humans (e.g., the Roman emperor), heavenly beings such as angels, or, most emphatically, other putative deities."[122] He thereby emphasizes "that this inclusion of Jesus as a second, distinguishable recipient of devotion is characteristically presented with a clear concern to avoid a simple di-theism, and to maintain a monotheistic stance, howbeit in an innovative form."[123]

This innovation has to be seen in an antagonistic mode, inasmuch as "[t]he 'monotheism' of ancient Jews and Christians was exhibited primarily in an avoidance of the *cultic worship* (as they practiced and understood it) of any other figure other than the biblical deity, i.e., sacrifice, prayer, ritual praise/ adoration, etc."[124] Paul himself had already warned very strictly against Christians' participation in sacred meals honoring pagan deities in his first letter to the Corinthians, and early believers attached great weight to these and similar warnings. According to Hurtado, this created a profound awareness, or indeed a devotion, and from there a practice of praying, that "produced ideas about God that involved some genuinely novel features. In particular, their efforts to affirm God's unity and uniqueness, while also according such a high status to Christ, produced a novel form of exclusivist monotheism."[125]

If Hurtado is right about this, and inasmuch as Bradshaw and Spinks are correct in rectifying things maintained by Jungmann and many other scholars in his wake, it can nevertheless be concluded that the doxological endings of the orations in the present Roman missal have astonishingly profound roots in the Christian tradition of prayer, devotion, and liturgy. The very DNA of the Church's *lex orandi*, which, as shown above in abundance, is undeniably marked by doxology, reveals a pattern of worship which not only respects an anterior form of monotheism, but which gives it a new shape. This new shape is Christic, which is probably a word which better captures what is at stake than the more often used categories of Christocentric or Christological.

---

[121] Larry W. Hurtado, "The Binitarian Pattern of Earliest Christian Devotion and Early Doctrinal Development," in Spinks, *The Place of Christ*, 27. Cf. also his pioneering monograph Larry W. Hurtado, *One God, One Lord: Early Christian Devotion and Ancient Jewish Monotheism* (London: SCM Press, 1988), and other related studies.

[122] Hurtado, "The Binitarian Pattern," 30.   [123] Hurtado, "The Binitarian Pattern," 32.

[124] Hurtado, "The Binitarian Pattern," 30.   [125] Hurtado, "The Binitarian Pattern," 50.

5 Myriad Saints and One True Savior: Exploring Their Connection

The question is now whether this Christic pattern of Christian monotheism can also be discovered and confirmed on the basis of an analysis of yet another important register of Christian liturgy, notably the veneration of the saints. The veneration of the saints has very deep roots in the Christian tradition. It is generally taken for granted that this practice had its roots in the cult of the martyrs at a time when Christian communities frequently found themselves under the imminent threat of persecutions in the Roman Empire, but also beyond.[126] After the time of these persecutions, which of course were not the only ones in history, the Church has continued to find outstanding examples of faith in the lives and fates of many people. Members of the Church have found comfort in these stories but also trust and teachings. They moreover have been convinced that they could connect themselves with them beyond the boundaries of death and that prayer is the most appropriate way to effectuate the connection.

However, in spite of its significance both for popular religiosity and for local history, there is usually very little attention for the veneration of the saints in academic theology. This relative silence is probably due, at least partially, to the painful memories about the harmful controversies about this issue around the time of the Reformation and afterwards. Catholics and Protestants entered into harsh debates with each other, developed theological positions about the intercession of the saints which were miles apart from each other, even opposing, and after a while they did not really listen to each other anymore and went their own ways.

The Catholic controversialist and Jesuit theologian Robert Bellarmine (1542–1621) very sharply understood what was at stake. On the one hand, he caricatured his Protestant opponents, imagined or not, when he said that "they have persuaded peoples that we hold dead men for the living God, worship bones, ashes, wood and stone in place of the supreme and eternal spirit," and that the consequence of insistently spreading that persuasion is that Catholic theologians like him "labor in not only an unjust but even grave and long lasting infamy."[127] On the other hand, Bellarmine rhetorically asked:

---

[126] This history is well documented in some of the key works of the famous Bollandist scholar Hippolyte Delehaye, *Les origines du culte des martyrs* (Brussels: Société des Bollandistes, 1912) and *Sanctus: Essai sur le culte des saints dans l'antiquité* (Brussels: Société des Bollandistes, 1927). Cf. also more recent works such as Peter Brown, *The Cult of the Saints: Its Rise and Function in Latin Christianity* (London and Chicago: Chicago University Press, 2014), originally dating from 1980, and Robert Bartlett, *Why Can the Dead Do Such Great Things? Saints and Worshippers from the Martyrs to the Reformation* (Princeton: Princeton University Press, 2015), with a stronger focus on medieval saints.

[127] Robert Bellarmine, *On the Canonization and Veneration of the Saints*, trans. Ryan Grant (Post Falls: Mediatrix Press, 2019), 2.

> Who in the Catholic Church offered the sacrifice due to the one God to saints, or relics or images? [...] Do we not clearly distinguish between that honor which is due to God alone, and that veneration which is piously and religiously granted to the friends of God and other sacred things on account of God himself?[128]

Bellarmine hoped to defuse some of the insults Protestants continued to direct at Catholics' invocation of the saints. Theologically he aimed at rectifying some of the mistaken judgments Protestants held about the Catholic practice of the veneration of the saints. In his own words, he wanted the saints' "glory" to be "known and respected through all the world and altogether vindicated, freed and resplendent from the fog of all idolatry."[129] So it seems that the tension between orthodoxy and idolatry was central to him in this context, and also that the issue of monotheism as seen through a doxological lens was at stake.

One of Bellarmine's main targets was John Calvin (1509–1564), who in his famous *Institutes* had argued vehemently against the cult of the saints. According to Calvin, the veneration of the saints was built on the false presumption that their intercessory prayer is to some extent effective for the salvation of humankind. This assumption moreover undermines the unique role of Christ in the divine economy. For Calvin it "is very clear without any doubt that all those who call upon God in another name than that of Jesus Christ disobey God's commandment and go against His will."[130] He added:

> As for the saints who are dead to this world but live with Christ, if we ascribe to them some prayer let us not dream that they have another way to pray than Christ who is the only way, or that their requests are accepted by God in another name.[131]

Paramount in Calvin's argumentation is his insistence on the unique mediatorship of Jesus Christ and, of course, the way in which that mediatorship is attested in Scripture. Calvin's major point of reference in this context is the passage in 1 Timothy 2:5 where Christ Jesus is called the "one mediator between God and humankind." Clearly, Calvin interprets this oneness in a strict and exclusive way: Christ does not share his mediatorship with anybody or anything else.

Intriguingly, it was this very same passage which turned out to be crucial for Jungmann, too. His reconstruction of orthodox Christian prayer in the early Church also rested, at least in terms of its biblical foundations, on 1 Timothy as a key reference. When it comes, then, to the veneration of the saints, which is the

---

[128] Bellarmine, *On the Canonization*, 6.   [129] Bellarmine, *On the Canonization*, 1.

[130] John Calvin, *Institutes of the Christian Religion: 1541 French Edition*, trans. Elsie Anne McKee (Grand Rapids and Cambridge: William B. Eerdmans, 2009), 467.

[131] Calvin, *Institutes*, 468.

subject of the last chapter of his abovementioned book, Jungmann highlights the tension which undeniably enters the scene when the martyrs and the saints are also believed to be somehow mediating between God and human beings. In this context, Jungmann refers to the fourth-century Church father Epiphanius of Salamis, who forcefully reacted against heresies and who held an overall dismissive attitude toward the commemoration of the saints. Jungmann summarizes his reasoning as follows: "if we give prominence to the intercession of the saints in our liturgical prayers, we put them on the same level with Christ, our unique Intercessor with God."[132]

The massive influence of the cult of the martyrs, however, steadily grew and thereby challenged theological convictions, ritual practices, and religious devotions. LaCugna observes a certain dogmatico-liturgical mechanism in early Christianity, which one can probably extrapolate to other geographical and historical contexts as well.

> As the mediatory role of Christ in his human nature became too doctrinally problematic to retain, and as the distinction between God and Christ became merely academic, veneration of the saints increased dramatically, since they in their humanity could provide the necessary bridge between us and God. This last development coincided with the growing devotion of Mary.[133]

Jungmann thinks it is helpful in this context to make a distinction between private and public worship. He supposes that addressing the saints was a phenomenon typical of private devotions, whereas official liturgical services did not regularly do this.[134] With the cautions raised by Spinks and Bradshaw in mind, one can respond to these assumptions that it is highly likely that the clear delineation of private prayer and public worship is very much something known to Jungmann from his own experience and that it is somewhat anachronistic to claim that it was as vigorously present then as it was in his own time. In other words, Jungmann may have had, at least at an implicit level, an apologetic

---

[132] Jungmann, *The Place of Christ*, 267.

[133] LaCugna, *God for Us*, 127. One could additionally say that Kearns further specifies the pattern of Mary's appearance in the Christian religion, inasmuch as she contends: "Mary comes to the fore – though in a highly qualified way – when and where the Eucharist is seen as a sacrifice in the strong sense [...], where there is emphasis on ritual transmission from generation to generation [...], and where there are tight hierarchical boundaries and sharp gender distinctions between clergy and laity [...]. When and where by contrast the Eucharist is seen as a sacrifice in the more diffuse sense [...], where there is less emphasis on ritual continuity and more on transmission through the word [...] and when there are more permeable, egalitarian boundaries and less sharp and gender sensitive distinctions between clergy and laity [...], Mary recedes from prominence and from any special or particular role in the eucharistic discourse." Kearns, *The Virgin Mary*, 268.

[134] Jungmann, *The Place of Christ*, 272: "The invocation of the saints directly addressed to them, as can be shown to have been practiced privately by the third century, has seldom been included among the prose prayers of the Mass liturgy."

agenda, notably to defend and promote official ecclesial liturgies over against what he considered mere devotions, and, in that context, to advance the Roman rite as exemplary.

> This meeting – especially in the Roman liturgy – with Christ the Lord, the Mediator between God and man, at all cross-roads, so to speak, is plainly characteristic of liturgical prayer in contrast to the free-growing, less restricted forms of popular piety.[135]

Someone who wrestled a lot with expressions of popular piety, both as a searching thinker and as a bishop responsible for the "care of souls" (*cura animarum*) of his people, was Augustine of Hippo. It is reported that the cult of the martyrs didn't play any role in his own conversion to Christianity, which it surely did in many other contemporary cases, and that he initially held a quite negative stance toward it.[136] As a matter of fact, as an intellectual, he rather looked down upon these practices, especially when memorial feasts of martyrs went along with excessive eating and drinking. In controversies in which he was involved later, however, he ardently defended the cult of the martyrs and, most interestingly, rebutted the idea that venerating the martyrs would in one way or another contradict Christian monotheism.

In his polemical writing *Contra Faustum Manichaeum*, Augustine refutes Faustus' reproach that Christians have simply replaced the pagan idols by their cult of saints.[137] Augustine admits that the Christian people indeed solemnly celebrate the memories of the martyrs, and that they do that to be inspired by their example, to connect themselves with what they have accomplished and to be helped by their prayer. But it is completely out of the question, Augustine emphasizes, that this implies that Christians would erect altars for the martyrs. Moreover, what is offered on those altars is for God only. The martyrs themselves, holy as they are, would be the first to resist the idea that it is to them that faithful bring offerings or build altars. Therefore, Augustine holds against Faustus that Christians do by no means either teach or practice a merging of the worship that is due to God only and the veneration of the martyrs.

What is noteworthy in this context is that Augustine twice refers to the Greek concept of *latreia*. He emphatically mentions that this Greek word cannot be

---

[135] Jungmann, *The Place of Christ*, 275.

[136] Tarcisius J. Van Bavel, "The Cult of the Martyrs in St. Augustine: Theology versus Popular Religion?" in *Martyrium in Multidisciplinary Perspective: Memorial Louis Reekmans*, ed. Mathijs Lamberigts and Peter Van Deun (Leuven: Peeters, 1995), 351–361. Cf. also an older but still valuable and very informative study, Frederik G. J. Van der Meer, *Augustine the Bishop: The Life and Work of a Father of the Church*, trans. Brian Battershaw and George R. Lamb (London and New York: Sheed & Ward, 1961), in particular chapter 17.

[137] Augustine of Hippo, *Contra Fastum Manichaeum*, XX.21.

rendered by one single concept in Latin. He explains *latreia* to be that form of worship – Augustine uses the word *cultus* – which is due to God only and connects it with the idea of sacrificing. He distinguishes between sacrificing for the martyrs and sacrificing for God in memory of, or on the day of the memorial feast of, the martyrs (*sacrificare Deo in memoriis martyrum*). Of the latter, he moreover says that this is what Christians often do and that it is perfectly in line with the New Testament and what it entails for the kind of adoration that is due to God alone (*quod pertinet ad illum cultum, quae latria dicitur, et uni Deo debetur*).[138]

Augustine did not contrast the concept of *latreia* with the one of *douleia* in this context, though it later became essential to theorize about the relationship between worshiping one God and Savior and venerating a sheer endless series of saints. As Thomas Thompson succinctly puts it in a chapter added to a famous manual on Mariology: "Adoration or worship (*latria*) is directed to the Triune God, an acknowledgement of total dependence which includes praise, thanksgiving and petition. In the Communion of Saints, veneration is directed to the Virgin Mary (*hyperdulia*) and to the saints (*dulia*)."[139]

Similar distinctions are made in the Catechism of the Catholic Church,[140] which in its turn relies on the authoritative teachings of the Second Vatican Council. In *Lumen gentium*, the council's constitution on the Church, it is said that the cult of Mary – but one could apply this to the cult of martyrs and saints as well – "differs essentially from the cult of adoration which is offered to the Incarnate Word, as to the Father and the Holy Spirit, and is most favorable to it."[141] Put differently, the veneration of Mary and the saints is auxiliary with respect to the worship of the one God, known to Christians as Father, Son, and Holy Spirit, and consequently neither threatens nor compromises in any way their monotheistic basic beliefs. To the contrary, the veneration of Mary and the saints is conducive to the worship of God.

---

[138] This patristic reading from book 20 of Augustine's *Contra Faustum* is scheduled in the office of readings in the Roman rite on the day when Pope Damasus I is commemorated, that is, on December 11. This late-fourth-century Church father is known to have been a fervent promoter of the cult of the martyrs.

[139] Hilda Graef, *Mary: A History of Doctrine and Devotion* (Notre Dame: Ave Maria Press, 2009), 424–425. From an etymological perspective, it is interesting to point out that both *latreia* and *douleia* evoke the idea of subjection, servitude, yes, even slavery.

[140] Cf. e.g., *Catechism of the Catholic Church*, #2132, where it speaks about the veneration for images of the saints, and where a quotation from Thomas Aquinas' *Summa Theologiae* is used to underline that adoration is due only to God. In #2141, the Catechism adds that the veneration of images does not contradict the first commandment.

[141] *Lumen gentium*, #66.

From an ecumenical perspective, Wainwright seems to concur with this, inasmuch as he concludes:

> Despite the iconoclasts of the eighth century and the *bilderstürmer* of the sixteenth, and despite persistent Protestant suspicion, the veneration of images and of saints has remained a feature of the broad Christian tradition. The dangers of this practice are real, and the periodic attacks and the constant questioning are therefore valuable and even necessary in view of sinful humanity's propensity to erect more "congenial" idols in place of the true God. Yet theology has in fact managed to suggest an understanding which in principle purges this religious pattern of its polytheistic origins and potentially idolatrous content by turning the worship in the direction of the true God who may be encountered *in* his saints or *in* given symbols.[142]

The liturgy itself, in its capacity of the Church's *lex orandi*, unambiguously confirms this. Three well-chosen examples from the Roman rite may suffice here. First, a reference to the solemnity of All Saints seems obvious, for it is the annual feast day, November 1, on which all the saints, and maybe even more the communion among them, are celebrated. A quick survey of the Mass orations for this feast teaches that a clear distinction is made between the celebrating community's attitude toward God and toward the saints. The opening prayer of the Eucharist on All Saints is as follows, and it has been that for centuries.[143] The prayer is a good example of one that is addressed to God the Father.

> Almighty ever-living God,
> by whose gift we venerate in one celebration
> the merits of all Saints,
> bestow on us, we pray,
> through the prayers of so many intercessors,
> an abundance of the reconciliation with you
> for which we earnestly long.
> Through our Lord Jesus Christ, your son,
> who lives and reigns with you in the unity of the Holy Spirit,
> one God, for ever and ever.[144]

It is assumed in this prayer that what the saints are doing is praying and that what they did during their lifetime was pleasing to God. The assembly utters the desire to somehow become sharers in the abundant divine graces in which the saints are already sharing in a more intense way, but in no way is God's unique divinity here questioned. The prayer after communion on All Saints

---

[142] Wainwright, *Doxology*, 59.

[143] The *collecta* prayer in use in the *Missale Romanum* prior to the liturgical reforms in line with Vatican II was exactly the same. By contrast, the prayer over the offerings and the prayer after communion are new, or at least newly inserted, compositions.

[144] *The Roman Missal*, 979.

corroborates this pattern, inasmuch as it explicitly refers to the abovementioned line from Revelation where it is said that God alone is holy.

> As we adore you, O God, who alone are holy
> and wonderful in all your Saints,
> we implore your grace,
> so that, coming to perfect holiness in the fullness of your love,
> we may pass from this pilgrim table
> to the banquet of our heavenly homeland.
> Through Christ our Lord.[145]

The Latin original makes it even more clear that it is God's holiness that is praised *in* the saints (*Mirabilem te, Deus, et unum Sanctum in omnibus Sanctis tuis adorantes*).[146] The saints are imagined to be in heaven and as such enjoying the heavenly banquet. The Church's Eucharistic celebration is in no way comparable to that feast, but the hope is expressed that the community of the faithful is on its way to it. The saints, whom the preface for the mass of All Saints calls "our sisters and brothers" as well as "exalted members of the Church,"[147] are the invitees at the banquet. However, there is no confusion whatsoever as to who invites. That is God only.

Second, one could take a closer look at the Roman canon, the Eucharistic prayer which has determined the identity of the Roman rite for about one and a half millennium, and which functioned as the sole anaphora until the reforms of the liturgy in the wake of Vatican II.[148] One of the distinctive features of that prayer is that it contains two enigmatic lists of saints, some of whom are hardly known today because there is virtually nothing that can be found about them with certainty in historical sources.[149] The first series of saints appears before the institution narrative and is known by its opening words *Communicantes*. The second one is situated toward the end of the text, that is, after the words of institution, and is a part of the section that starts with the words *Nobis quoque (peccatoribus)*. Both these parts are supposed to have been added later and are traditionally attributed to Gelasius I, who was the pope at the end of the fifth century CE (492–496).[150]

In both cases, an appeal is made to "your Apostles and Martyrs," who are respectfully considered "blessed" (in the *Communicantes*) and "holy" (in the *Nobis Quoque*). In the *Communicantes*, what is being expressed is that the celebrating assembly puts itself in communion with persons whose faithful lives (and deaths) are commemorated with particular reverence. Among these persons are

---

[145] *The Roman Missal*, 982.   [146] *Missale Romanum*, 858.   [147] *The Roman Missal*, 981.

[148] Mazza, *The Celebration of the Eucharist*, 269–271.

[149] Charles L. Feltoe, "The Saints Commemorated in the Roman Canon," *The Journal of Theological Studies* 15 (1914) 226–235.

[150] Jasper and Cuming, *Prayers of the Eucharist*, 159.

the twelve apostles,[151] followed by an equal number of martyrs who have a special significance for the Church of Rome. This list of twenty-four illustrious figures is headed by Mary and Joseph, who are the only ones receiving further qualifications in the text. Mary is reverently called "the glorious ever-Virgin" and "Mother of our God and Lord, Jesus Christ"[152] – we have seen above what is so special about the equation of God and Lord in Christian liturgy and its attempt at remaining as monotheistic as the Jewish tradition it received. The mention of Saint Joseph, "her Spouse," is something that was instituted by Pope John XXIII,[153] who not only had a special person devotion for Jesus' foster father but who also placed the Second Vatican Council under his protection in his capacity of patron saint of the world church.

The second series of saints in the *Nobis quoque* section of the Roman canon reinforces a pure monotheism insofar as there is not the least tendency toward a blurring of God's unique divinity with (very special) human beings' holiness. This second list is headed by John the Baptist, in whose wake the names of seven male and seven female martyrs follow. Among them are famous ones like "protomartyr" Stephen, who according to the New Testament was stoned (Acts 7:54–60), Ignatius of Antioch, Felicity and Perpetua, and Cecilia, but also more obscure ones like Marcellinus and Anastasia. What is asked for in the anaphora, notably "through Christ our Lord,"[154] is that the ones praying it may have a share in God's graces, realizing how partial and imperfect that will always be on earth. In other words, there is not the slightest intention to voice compromising things about God's uniqueness and divine being.

Third, it is instructive to refer to the liturgical celebration on the occasion of a canonization. This is normally a solemn papal mass in Saint Peter's basilica at Rome, which only takes place after a long and often arduous process, of which it is to some extent the apex. The fact itself that it is a Eucharistic celebration is an important element, meaning that other considerations pertaining to the liturgy in general apply. In particular, it is reasonable to suppose that the (Catholic) Church's monotheistic faith is not put at risk in one very specific kind of celebration. Moreover, during a Eucharist in which one or more new saints are proclaimed and thereby officially recognized, there is a rite where the community of the faithful, usually represented by the prefect of the Congregation for the Causes of Saints, solemnly requests the pope to include

---

[151] Intriguingly, in this list of the twelve apostles, Judas Iscariot is not replaced by Matthias (cf. Acts 1:26). Instead Paul is mentioned immediately after Peter, which is, of course, of particular relevance for Rome.

[152] *The Roman Missal*, 636; OM, #86.

[153] Mazza, *The Eucharistic Prayers of the Roman Rite*, 66, 299–300.

[154] *The Roman Missal*, 642; OM, #96.

henceforth in the Church's records one or more added persons among the saints. This rite underscores the profoundly human part in canonization processes, which in no way endanger or cast doubt on either God's divinity or uniqueness.

Other important elements of the ritual of a canonization are the singing of the Te Deum, which was discussed above, expressing joy and jubilation, and the litany of saints, expressing the dire needs of the Christian community. The litany of saints is a remarkable liturgical unit in the history of the Church, as it appears in the Roman rite in the celebration of the sacrament of baptism and ordinations as well as in the liturgical year, most prominently in the Easter vigil.[155] It thus, most interestingly, crosses different registers of liturgical activity and can therefore meaningfully speak to our topic.

The text of the litany, which varies a lot in terms of saints who can be mentioned, has nevertheless had a stable core for many centuries.[156] In essence, it is an extended petition to Christ, who is confessed to be Lord indeed. It starts with the threefold entreaty *Kyrie eleison – Christe eleison – Kyrie eleison*. Closeness to him and his work of redemption is thereupon presumed by appealing to many saints. Again, as was the case in the Roman canon, Jesus' mother and John the Baptist, his precursor, figure prominently at the top of the list. Other New Testament saints, including Joseph, Peter, Paul, Mary Magdalene, and Stephen follow; then come martyrs of the early Church, outstanding teachers in the faith, founders of religious congregations, missionaries, mystics, and so on. The whole point of appealing to all these personalities is the enhancing of the praying people's cry to be heard by "Jesus, Son of the living God" and "Lord." The litany terminates in exactly the same way as it began, that is, with supplications addressed to Christ: "hear us," "graciously hear us."

It would no doubt require more historical research and finer theological argumentation, but it makes a lot of sense to see in the pattern observed both in the Roman canon and in the litany of saints a parallel with the *deesis* icon in Byzantine Christianity. *Deesis* literally means supplication or entreaty, and refers to depictions of the heavenly Christ, that is, Christ in a mandorla and/or on a throne, with his mother Mary on his right-hand side and John the Baptist at his left. Mary and John are standing and hold their hands in an imploring position. Their gaze is humble and invites the spectator, which in the case of icons is actually always a meditator, to keep one's prayers directed to Christ, God. Sometimes, the *deesis* icon forms the center of a whole *deesis* row, for

---

[155] *The Roman Missal*, 370–373.

[156] For a more elaborate commentary, see Joris Geldhof, "The Litany of Saints of the Easter Vigil in the Roman Rite," in *The Litany in Arts and Cultures*, ed. Witold Sadowski and Francesco Marschiani (Turnhout: Brepols, 2020), 175–195.

example, on iconostases in church buildings. The row is then completed with a whole series of saints. All of them are supposed – and that is exactly why they are venerated, but not worshiped as one worships God – to have gone before where worshipers are going now and, each in their own way, to have kept their eyes and their prayers consistently and exemplarily on the one and true Lord.

Conclusion

The conclusion of this Element can be brief and consist of two major lines of thought which have run through it. First and foremost, it has been shown that the liturgy is an unsuspectedly rich, but grossly unexploited, quarry in which to learn a great deal about the Christian understanding of God. Both in terms of its ritual nature and in terms of its being the Church's preferred and privileged prayer, that is, both qua words and qua deeds, the liturgical celebrations of Christians allow a unique insight into how they conceive of God's uniqueness, divinity, and sanctity. If anything, this is an active and dynamic divinity. It has and keeps a fully transcendent nature, but it is at the same time one that is communicated to humankind with the specific purpose to make it participate in this formidable state of blessedness. Christian monotheism is uniquely qualified by the liturgy to the extent that it concretizes in myriad ways the profound awareness that the sole initiative to proclaim and make humanity share in God's grand work of salvation and redemption is God's own.

Second, it became manifest that, to understand how all of this works, the pervading impact of doxology on the entirety of Christian worship was the key. Here, too, liturgy further qualifies Christians' monotheistic beliefs. God is the only one worthy of worship, and God, that means Father, Son, and Holy Spirit for Christians. The pattern whereby Jesus Christ, the Son of God, is fully and unreservedly included in the worship of God the Father, primarily through naming and considering both divine persons Lord, and through doing that always in the unity of the Holy Spirit, seemed absolutely crucial. It can thus be said that it is above all through a doxological lens that it becomes comprehensible that there is no tension between the kind of monotheism that emerged and developed in Semitic culture as exemplified in the Old Testament on the one hand and the Trinitarian faith of Christians on the other. In addition, doxology and doxologies shed an interesting light on what orthodoxy for Christians means and how the continuous risk of idolatry can be avoided. Perhaps it is not an exaggeration to say that doxology is ultimately the most appropriate entry into the world of Christian monotheism.

References

The documents of the Second Vatican Council can be consulted in different languages on the Vatican's website: www.vatican.va/archive/hist_councils/ii_vati can_council/index.htm. The texts of other documents from the magisterium, such as encyclicals and post-synodal apostolic exhortations, but also the Catechism of the Catholic Church, can be easily found on the website of the Vatican, too.

Ashe, Geoffrey. *The Virgin: Mary's Cult and the Re-emergence of the Goddess* (London: Arkana, 1988).

Bartlett, Robert. *Why Can the Dead Do Such Great Things? Saints and Worshippers from the Martyrs to the Reformation* (Princeton: Princeton University Press, 2015).

Bellarmine, Robert. *On the Canonization and Veneration of the Saints*, trans. Ryan Grant (Post Falls: Mediatrix Press, 2019).

Benedictine Daily Prayer: A Short Breviary, compiled and ed. Maxwell E. Johnson (Dublin: The Columba Press, 2005).

Bouyer, Louis. *Eucharist: Theology and Spirituality of the Eucharistic Prayer*, trans. Charles Underhill Quinn (Notre Dame: University of Notre Dame Press, 2006 [1968]).

Bradshaw, Paul F. *Daily Prayer in the Early Church: A Study of the Origin and Early Development of the Divine Office* (London: SPCK, 1981).

Bradshaw, Paul F., and Johnson, Maxwell E. *The Eucharistic Liturgies: Their Evolution and Interpretation* (Collegeville: Liturgical Press, 2012).

Bradshaw, Paul F., Johnson, Maxwell E., and Philips, L. Edward. *The Apostolic Tradition: A Commentary* (Minneapolis: Fortress Press, 2002).

Brown, Peter. *The Cult of the Saints: Its Rise and Function in Latin Christianity* (London and Chicago: Chicago University Press, 2014).

Callewaert, Camille. "La finale du canon de la messe," *Revue d'histoire ecclésiastique* 39 (1943) 5–21.

Calvin, John. *Institutes of the Christian Religion: 1541 French Edition*, trans. Elsie Anne McKee (Grand Rapids and Cambridge: William B. Eerdmans, 2009).

Cappelle, Bernard. "Le texte du 'Gloria in excelsis'," *Revue d'histoire ecclésiastique* 44 (1949) 439–457.

Casel, Odo. *The Mystery of Christian Worship*, ed. Burkhard Neunheuser (New York: The Crossroad, 1999).

Clément, Olivier. *The Roots of Christian Mysticism: Text and Commentary* (London, Dublin, and Edinburgh: New City Press, 2002).

Collin, Matthieu. *Comme un murmure de cithare: Introduction aux Psaumes* (Paris and Perpignan: Desclée de Brouwer, 2007).

Congar, Yves. *Je crois en l'Esprit Saint* (Paris: Cerf, 1997).

Crichton, James D. *Christian Celebration: The Prayer of the Church* (London: Geoffrey Chapman, 1976).

Cullmann, Oscar. *Early Christian Worship*, trans. A. Stewart Todd and James B. Torrance (London: SCM Press, 1969 [1953]).

Davies, Brian. *Thomas Aquinas's* Summa Theologiae*: A Guide and Commentary* (Oxford: Oxford University Press, 2014).

De Kesel, Marc. *Goden breken: Essays over monotheïsme* (Amsterdam: Boom, 2010).

Delehaye, Hippolyte. *Les origines du culte des martyrs* (Brussels: Société des Bollandistes, 1912).

   Sanctus: Essai sur le culte des saints dans l'antiquité (Brussels: Société des Bollandistes, 1927).

Fagerberg, David W. *Consecrating the World: On Mundane Liturgical Theology* (Kettering: Angelico Press, 2016).

Feltoe, Charles L. "The Saints Commemorated in the Roman Canon," *The Journal of Theological Studies* 15 (1914) 226–235.

Fischer, Balthasar. "Le Christ dans les psaumes: La dévotion aux psaumes dans l'Église des martyrs," *La Maison-Dieu* 27 (1951) 86–113.

Geldhof, Joris. "Liturgical Theology," *Oxford Research Encyclopedia of Religion* (2015). https://oxfordre.com/religion/view/10.1093/acrefore/9780199340378.001.0001/acrefore-9780199340378-e-14.

   Liturgical Theology as a Research Program (Leiden and Boston: Brill, 2020).

Gerhards, Albert. "Te Deum laudamus – Die Marseillaise der Kirche? Ein christlicher Hymnus im Spannungsfeld von Liturgie und Politik," *Liturgisches Jarhbuch* 40 (1990) 65–77.

Giraudo, Cesare. *In unum corpus: Traité mystagogique sur l'Eucharistie*, trans. Éric Iborra and Pierre-Marie Hombert (Paris: Cerf, 2014).

Graef, Hilda. *Mary: A History of Doctrine and Devotion* (Notre Dame: Ave Maria Press, 2009).

Hurtado, Larry W. *One God, One Lord: Early Christian Devotion and Ancient Jewish Monotheism* (London: SCM Press, 1988).

Hyatt, J. Philip. "Yehezkel Kaufmann's View of the Religion of Israel," *Journal of Bible and Religion* 29 (1961) 52–27.

Irwin, Kevin W. *Context and Text: A Method for Liturgical Theology*, rev. ed. (Collegeville: Liturgical Press, 2018).

Jasper, Ronald C. D., and Cuming, Geoffrey J. *Prayers of the Eucharist: Early and Reformed*, 3rd ed. (Collegeville: Liturgical Press, 1990).

Jeggle-Merz, Birgit, Kirchschläger, Walter, and Müller, Jörg, eds. *Gemeinsam vor Gott treten: Die Liturgie mit biblischen Augen betrachten*, Luzerner Biblisch-Liturgischer Kommentar zum Ordo Missae, vol. 1 (Stuttgart: Katholisches Bibelwerk, 2014).

Jungmann, Joseph Andreas. *The Mass of the Roman Rite: Its Origins and Development (Missarum Sollemnia)*, 2 vols. (Notre Dame: Ave Maria Press, 2012).

The Place of Christ in Liturgical Prayer (London: Geoffrey Chapman, 1989).

Kaufmann, Yehezkel. *The Religion of Israel: From its Beginnings to the Babylonian Exile*, trans. Moshe Greenberg (London: George Allen & Unwin, 1961).

Kavanagh, Aidan. *On Liturgical Theology* (Collegeville: Liturgical Press, 1992).

Kiesgen, Agape. "Die große Doxologie der Kirche," *Bibel und Liturgie* 2 (1927/1928) 273–279, 320–326.

LaCugna, Catherine Mowry. "Can Liturgy Ever Again Be a Source for Theology," *Studia Liturgica* 19 (1989) 1–13.

God for Us: The Trinity and Christian Life (San Francisco: Harper Collins, 1991).

Lamberigts, Mathijs, and Van Deun, Peter, eds. *Martyrium in Multidisciplinary Perspective: Memorial Louis Reekmans* (Leuven: Peeters, 1995).

LaVerdiere, Eugene. *The Eucharist in the New Testament and the Early Church* (Collegeville: Liturgical Press, 1996).

Lohfink, Gerhard. *Prayer Takes Us Home: The Theology and Practice of Christian Prayer*, trans. Linda M. Maloney (Collegeville: Liturgical Press, 2020).

Mazza, Enrico. *The Celebration of the Eucharist: The Origins of the Rite and the Development of Its Interpretation*, trans. Matthew J. O'Connell (Collegeville: Liturgical Press, 1999).

The Eucharistic Prayers of the Roman Rite, trans. Matthew J. O'Connell (Collegeville: Liturgical Press, 2004).

McNelly Kearns, Cleo. *The Virgin Mary, Monotheism, and Sacrifice* (Cambridge: Cambridge University Press, 2008).

Missale Romanum, editio typica tertia, reimpressio emendata (Città del Vaticano: Libreria Editrice Vaticana, 2008).

Sadowski, Witold, and Marschiani, Francesco, eds. *The Litany in Arts and Cultures* (Turnhout: Brepols, 2020)

Saliers, Don E. *Worship as Theology: Foretaste of Glory Divine* (Nashville: Abingdon Press, 1994).

Schmemann, Alexander. *Introduction to Liturgical Theology*, trans. Asheleigh E. Moorehouse (Crestwood: Saint Vladimir's Seminary Press, 2003 [1966]).

Liturgy and Tradition: Theological Reflections of Alexander Schmemann, ed. Thomas Fisch (New York: Saint Vladimir's Seminary Press, 1990).

Spinks, Bryan D., ed. *The Place of Christ in Liturgical Prayer: Trinity, Christology, and Liturgical Theology* (Collegeville: Liturgical Press, 2008).

Taft, Robert. *The Liturgy of the Hours in East and West: The Origins of the Divine Office and its Meaning for Today*, 2nd rev. ed. (Collegeville: Liturgical Press, 1993).

The Liturgy Documents: A Parish Resource, vol. 2 (Chicago: Liturgy Training Publications, 1999).

The Roman Missal, English translation according to the third typical edition (Collegeville: Liturgical Press, 2011).

Tück, Jan-Heiner. *Gabe der Gegenwart: Theologie und Dichtung der Eucharistie bei Thomas von Aquin* (Freiburg, Basel, and Wien: Herder, 2009).

Vagaggini, Cipriano. *Theological Dimensions of the Liturgy: A General Treatise on the Theology of Liturgy*, trans. Leonard J. Doyle and William A. Jurgens (Collegeville: Liturgical Press, 1976).

Van der Meer, Frederik G. J. *Augustine the Bishop: The Life and Work of a Father of the Church*, trans. Brian Battershaw and George R. Lamb (London and New York: Sheed & Ward, 1961).

Vergote, Antoon. *Cultuur, religie, geloof* (Leuven: Universitaire Pers Leuven, 1989).

De Heer je God liefhebben: Het eigene van het christendom (Tielt: Lannoo, 1999).

Wainwright, Geoffrey. *Doxology: The Praise of God in Worship, Doctrine, and Life: A Systematic Theology* (New York: Oxford University Press, 1980).

Wolterstorff, Nicholas. *The God We Worship: An Exploration of Liturgical Theology* (Grand Rapids and Cambridge: William B. Eerdmans, 2015).

Cambridge Elements ⹀

Religion and Monotheism

Paul K. Moser
Loyola University Chicago

Paul K. Moser is Professor of Philosophy at Loyola University Chicago. He is the author of *Paul's Gospel of Divine Self-Sacrifice; The Divine Goodness of Jesus; Divine Guidance; Understanding Religious Experience; The God Relationship; The Elusive God* (winner of national book award from the Jesuit Honor Society); *The Evidence for God; The Severity of God; Knowledge and Evidence* (all Cambridge University Press); and *Philosophy after Objectivity* (Oxford University Press); co-author of *Theory of Knowledge* (Oxford University Press); editor of *Jesus and Philosophy* (Cambridge University Press) and *The Oxford Handbook of Epistemology* (Oxford University Press); co-editor of *The Wisdom of the Christian Faith* (Cambridge University Press). He is the co-editor with Chad Meister of the book series *Cambridge Studies in Religion, Philosophy, and Society*.

Chad Meister
Affiliate Scholar, Ansari Institute for Global Engagement with Religion, University of Notre Dame

Chad Meister is Affiliate Scholar at the Ansari Institute for Global Engagement with Religion at the University of Notre Dame. His authored and co-authored books include *Evil: A Guide for the Perplexed* (Bloomsbury Academic, 2nd edition); *Introducing Philosophy of Religion* (Routledge); *Introducing Christian Thought* (Routledge, 2nd edition); and *Contemporary Philosophical Theology* (Routledge). He has edited or co-edited the following: *The Oxford Handbook of Religious Diversity* (Oxford University Press); *Debating Christian Theism* (Oxford University Press); with Paul Moser, *The Cambridge Companion to the Problem of Evil* (Cambridge University Press); and with Charles Taliaferro, *The History of Evil* (Routledge, in six volumes). He is the co-editor with Paul Moser of the book series *Cambridge Studies in Religion, Philosophy, and Society*.

About the Series

This Cambridge Element series publishes original concise volumes on monotheism and its significance. Monotheism has occupied inquirers since the time of the Biblical patriarch, and it continues to attract interdisciplinary academic work today. Engaging, current, and concise, the Elements benefit teachers, researched, and advanced students in religious studies, Biblical studies, theology, philosophy of religion, and related fields.

Cambridge Elements ≡

Religion and Monotheism

Elements in the Series

Hindu Monotheism
Gavin Dennis Flood

Monotheism and the Rise of Science
J. L. Schellenberg

Monotheism and Faith in God
Ian G. Wallis

Monotheism and Human Nature
Andrew M. Bailey

Monotheism and Forgiveness
S. Mark Heim

Monotheism, Biblical Traditions, and Race Relations
Yung Suk Kim

Monotheism and Existentialism
Deborah Casewell

Monotheism, Suffering, and Evil
Michael L. Peterson

Necessary Existence and Monotheism: An Avicennian Account of the Islamic Conception of Divine Unity
Mohammad Saleh Zarepour

Islam and Monotheism
Celene Ibrahim

Freud's Monotheism
William Parsons

Monotheism in Christian Liturgy
Joris Geldhof

A full series listing is available at: www.cambridge.org/er&m

Lightning Source UK Ltd.
Milton Keynes UK
UKHW020258080223
416610UK00016B/2060

9 781009 001847